THE IRISH

W9-BAJ-544

THE IRISH

Photographs by Andrew M. Greeley
...Along with Poems, Proverbs, and Blessings

ANDREW M. GREELEY

CB
CONTEMPORARY
BOOKS
CHICAGO

Library of Congress Cataloging-in-Publication Data

Greeley, Andrew M., 1928–
    The Irish : photographs by Andrew M. Greeley—along with poems,
proverbs, and blessings / Andrew M. Greeley.
        p.   cm.
    ISBN 0-8092-4287-7 (cloth)
            0-8092-3964-7 (paper)
    1. Irish Americans—Pictorial works.   2. Ireland—Description
and
travel—1981–   Views.   I. Title.
E184.I6G724   1990
779′.9973049162—dc20

90-1994
CIP

All photographs, prose, and poems
except where otherwise noted are the
work of Andrew M. Greeley

Copyright © 1990 by Andrew Greeley Enterprises
All rights reserved
Published by Contemporary Books, Inc.
180 North Michigan Avenue, Chicago, Illinois 60601
Manufactured in the United States of America
International Standard Book Number: 0-8092-4287-7 (cloth)
                                        0-8092-3964-7 (paper)

I dedicate these pages
to my Guardian Angel,
impressing upon her
that I am only fooling
and warning her
to see to it that
there is no misunderstanding
when I go home.

(adapted from Flan O'Brien, who didn't realize that guardian angels are mostly women angels—rather like Irish mothers, wives, and daughters, come to think of it)

I am of Ireland,
And of the holy Land
Of Ireland.
Good Sir, pray I thee,
For of *saint charité*
Come dance with me
In Ireland.

—Anonymous, fourteenth century

The Irish have captured the world's imagination, and the game of interpreting them has been going on for centuries, often with doubtful results.

—Anonymous

Contents

⊛ THE IRISH ⊛

I
Introduction

BALLENDREHID

Grandpa walked down this winding track,
Left the white stone house where his life began,
Squared his thin shoulders, never once looked back,
The second son no one would see again.
The firstborn stayed here, lucky, on the farm,
Wrestled life from this stern and soggy ground,
Enjoyed the stone fences and home's familiar charm,
Mourned for early death, all his brother found.

His quiet, gentle offspring still work the land,
A hard task but healthy folk and strong,
Their life prospects, I fear, not exactly grand,
Unneurotic, they know where they belong.
Sorry, cousins, I'm from beyond the sea;
Poor, sad Grandpa; affluent, lucky me.

THE LAND CALLED SCOTIA

It is said that western land is of Earth the best,
that land called by name 'Scotia' in the ancient books:
an island rich in goods, jewels, cloth, and gold,
benign to the body, mellow in soil and air.
The plains of lovely Ireland flow with honey and milk.
There are clothes and fruit and arms and art in plenty;
no bears in ferocity there, nor any lions,
for the land of Ireland never bore their seed.
No poisons pain, no snakes slide in the grass,
nor does the chattering frog groan on the lake.
And a people dwell in that land who deserve their home,
a people renowned in war and peace and faith.

—St. Donatus, the first bishop of Fiesoli,
fifth century

THE COUNTY MAYO

Now with the coming in of the spring the days will stretch a bit,
And after the Feast of Brigid I shall hoist my flag and go,
For since the thought got into my head I can neither stand nor sit
Until I find myself in the middle of the County of Mayo.

In Claremorris I would stop a night and sleep with decent men,
And then go on to Balla just beyond and drink galore,
And next to Kiltimagh for a visit of about a month, and then
I would only be a couple of miles away from Ballymore.

I say and swear my heart lifts up like the lifting of a tide,
Rising up like the rising wind till fog or mist must go,
When I remember Carra and Gallen close beside,
And the Gap of the Two Bushes, and the wide plains of Mayo.

To Killaden then, to the place where everything grows that is best,
There are raspberries there and strawberries there
and all that is good for men;
And if I were only there in the middle of my folk my heart could rest,
For age itself would leave me there and I'd be young again.

—From the Irish of Raftery,
late eighteenth century

You are now leaving the County Mayo.
Last one out please turn off the lights.
(And first one in tomorrow please light the fire!)

—Sign on the border of Mayo

Sure, don't I know who you are?
You're the third-best theologian
in the County Mayo!

—Remark of woman newsagent to
Maynooth theologian

May the morning sun stir you out of bed
May the winter winds move you on the road
May the rains of March renew your strength
May the flowers of spring captivate your sight
May summer heat inflame your zeal
May autumn color stimulate your dreams
May the silver moon make you wiser yet
May you never be with yourself content
May Jesus and Mary keep you young
Full of life and laughter and love

And may the God of challenge and adventure
Bless you and keep you always
Father, Son, and Holy Spirit

"May you have a good trip," the old man said.
His smile, directions given, chased the rain.
Red-faced, he tipped the cap on his silver head,
Softly prayed that God would bring me back again.
And the colleen small at an open door,
"Ah, sure, a bit you must eat and stay awhile."
They give all they have and something more,
Catch you in the warmth of an Irish smile.

If of Celtic charm you've had not enough,
Go to Glenbeigh road for music and the dance.
Welcomes flow as a stream in springtime flood.
Recall Paddy Reilly to Ballyjamesduff,
Hear a singing bishop, your final chance;
Can't stop, poor folk, it's in their Irish blood.

This book is a celebration of the Irish condition as it is found in both Ireland and the United States. In celebrating the Irish—and their distinctive faces—I do not intend to suggest that I think the Irish are better than anyone else. Nor do I mean to imply that they are totally different from anyone else. My thesis is much more modest. The Irish are a little bit different from other people, and that difference is worth enjoying and celebrating.

'Tis a terrible fate to be Irish, I might quietly add, till one considers the alternatives.

And just how are the Irish different? To answer that I'd like to delve briefly into some Irish history and then talk with you about the truths and nontruths of stereotypes. But first, of course, I'll be wanting to tell you a story. Please allow me my exuberances—of sociologist, of storyteller, of priest—in this book of the Irish.

The story comes from another tradition—perhaps from every other tradition—but it is here adapted to fit the Irish tradition. As with most stories, 'tis the telling of it that's more important than the story itself. You must imagine that this story is told with a strong (and phony) Irish brogue.

Once upon a time St. Colum, the holy abbot of Iona, and himself also known as Columcille, was sitting in front of his beehive hut. His eyes were closed, as they often were. Some folks said he was praying. Other folks said he was sleeping. Still others said, well, sure, if he's a saint, can't he do both?

Anyway, every day when he came out of the beehive hut he brought with him the pile of stones he'd collected—your man Colum was a great one for collecting stones when he walked along the strand—and deposited them next to where he was sleeping or praying or doing whatever he was doing.

Well, one day, along about noontime, the saint having his eyes closed and the rain falling only lightly and the pile of stones glittering in the rain, who should ride up on his great black horse and his wolfhounds trailing behind but Rory O'Neill himself, the Ard-ri, the High King of all Ireland?

The horse huffed and puffed, and the wolfhounds gamboled around and barked, and the king's courtiers reined in their own mounts, and the king's wife, Queen Fionna, pulled up her own milk-white horse and frowned a little bit because she thought that himself was a little bit too impulsive for his own good—which of course is what every Irish wife has thought since the beginning of the human race, if not before, and will think until at least the day after the Last Judgment.

"Abbot Colum," says your man, dismounting from his black horse and speaking real business-like, "I've come to take one of your stones."

"Have you now?" says the holy man, opening one eye.

"Haven't I said so?" says the king.

(You must understand that usually the Irish end their sentences with question marks.)

" 'Tis a stone you want?" says the abbot.

"Hasn't the holy Archangel Michael himself come to me in a dream and told me that I would find in your pile a stone that would bring me victory and success and power and wealth and happiness?"

"Has he now?"

"Haven't I said so? And is it yourself that would deny a request from the High King of Ireland and himself your cousin?"

"Sure, would I ever do a thing like that?"

"Well," says the king, searching through the pile, "wouldn't the magic stone be this gorgeous ruby right here on the top of the pile?"

"Hmm . . . " said the holy abbot, resting his eyes a bit.

It bothered the High King's conscience a wee tad to be after taking such a gorgeous stone.

"Is it this one now?" he asked the holy abbot.

The abbot opened up one eye. "Ah, is that the one you'd be wanting?"

" 'Tis," said the High King.

"Sure, why wouldn't you be taking it"—the abbot picked up the gem and put it in the king's hand—"and meself only finding it yesterday and having no use for such a thing anyway, would I now?"

So the king took the stone, mounted his horse, and rode off, followed by his courtiers and his barking wolfhounds. The queen stayed behind a bit to watch the abbot. Even she couldn't tell whether he was sleeping or praying—and let me tell you, herself didn't miss much at all, at all.

Well, the king was quiet when they got back to the ranch in Tara, and there was not much of the drink taken that night, let me tell you.

The king merely sat on his throne and stared, kind of blank-like, at the ruby. He didn't move all night long. The queen, who knew your man's moods pretty well, finally said to him, "Och, Rory, you eejit, you're going to have to go back first thing in the morning and see the holy abbot again, aren't you now?"

"Woman," says the king with a loud sigh, "I am."

"Haven't you been a terrible amadon altogether?" she says, never one to miss making that point when it needed to be made.

"I have," says the king.

Well, the first thing in the morning, doesn't the king saddle up his black horse and ride back to the strand and to the abbot's beehive hut?

"I'm bringing back your ruby," your man says.

The abbot opened one eye, not the one he'd opened the day before but the other one. "Aren't you after wanting that stone?" he says.

"I do not," says the king. "I am after wanting the magic stone."

"And what one is that?" The abbot opened his other eye.

"The one that enabled you to give away this precious gem with such charming and gracious generosity. That's the stone I must have."

Now, putting on my sociologist's hat, I must make two observations. First, I believe cultural traits survive the immigration experience and even the experience of ethnic intermarriage. My argument is not that all such traits survive or that the Irish-Americans and the real Irish (or the Italian-Americans and the real Italians) are the same. But there are similarities between emigrants and natives that justify our talking about them as though they were, under some circumstances, the same group.

Second, when one talks about various ethnic traits, one does not say that everyone in an ethnic group possesses these traits and that no one in other ethnic groups possesses them. One rather asserts a probability—for instance, on the average the Irish are more likely to be tolerant than certain other groups and, on the average, they are more likely to be politically involved, and therefore politically skilled, than other groups. All stereotypes, my friend Professor Sidney Verba once remarked, are 30 percent true. That's enough to make the traits "stereotypes."

There are, God knows, Irish bigots, and far too many of them. And there are Irish who are not interested in politics, which is surely their privilege (though 'tis a bit strange, don't you think?). There are even Irish who don't drink much, and there are not enough of them.

And not all Irish wives are as convinced of the adolescent impulsiveness of their men as is Queen Fionna in my story. I'm sure there are some Irish wives who don't think that at all. Mind you, I haven't met any of them.

Sociologically speaking, the traits I will celebrate in this book—in addition to the faces, which are the real cause for celebration—are, then, propensities, tendencies, inclinations, modest correlations.

Mind you, not all the stereotypes are true, even 30 percent true. Contrary to the liberal stereotype of the Irish as bigots, statistics show that the Irish are the most tolerant gentile ethnic group in America. Other data also show that the Irish are the most tolerant people in the English-speaking world. Here's another stereotype shattered: when the common market was only nine nations, Ireland was sixth out of the nine in per-capita consumption of alcohol. And Irish-Americans do not have the highest alcoholism rates of American groups. (I won't trouble you with information about which group has the highest rate, as it is irrelevant to this story.) Also contrary to popular belief, the Irish-Americans are the best-educated gentile group in the United States; and the real Irish have the highest per-capita book consumption rate in the world, as well as the highest home ownership rate in Europe.

So there'll be nothing in this book about the heavy drinking, hard-fighting, semiliterate Irish. There are such, God knows, but we have no reason to be proud of them, and we do not have a disproportionate share of them either. The stereotypes aren't true.

What, then, does make the Irish different? The roots are found, I believe, in important, unique historical experiences. First of all, they're not quite European. Much of what shaped the Europe of today—the Renaissance, the Reformation, the French Revolution, the Industrial Revolution—never happened in Ireland; or if it did happen, it didn't have the impact it did elsewhere on the Continent. Hence Ireland has stronger and more direct links to its archaic past than do other European nations. English poet laureate John Betjeman expressed this truth in a poem that, I think, was meant to be a put-down of the Irish:

> Stony seaboard, far and foreign,
> Stony hills poured over space,
> Stony outcrop of the Burren
> Stones in every fertile place,
> Little fields with boulders dotted
> Gray-stone shoulders saffron-spotted,
> Stone-walled cabins thatched with reeds,
> Where a Stone Age people breeds
> The last of Europe's Stone Age race.

> *—from "Sunday in Ireland"*

Last Stone Age race, huh? Better to say that Ireland is the only country in Western Europe that still has contact with its archaic origins—in both its serious literature and its ordinary life. It is through this relatively clear channel to the past that one finds, I believe, the nature mysticism that shaped Irish poets in the monasteries of long ago and the Ulster poets of today, most notably the great Seamus Heaney. It is in the prehistory of Ireland too that one finds the Irish comic tradition, the love of language, and the combination of the two in endless wit. That wit survives admirably today. For example:

Several years ago American Express gave the people of Ireland a bust of James Joyce—poor Jimmy Joyce at last honored in Dublin but by the frigging Yanks. Aye, but when it was unveiled by the Uactharan na h'Eireann (the president of Ireland) in St. Stephen's Green, a loud voice in the crowd announced almost instantly, "The next time, let's try Visa."

Similarly the statue of Molly Malone at the head of Grafton Street was promptly called "the tart with the cart" because of Molly's delightful cleavage.

And in celebration of its millennium, the fair city received another important gift, a statue of Anna Livia Plurabelle—James Joyce's wordplay on the river Liffey, once called the Anna Liffey—and she was immediately dubbed "the floozie in the Jacuzzi."

This wit, I submit, would be possible only in a people whose age-old poetry and humor (often ribald) had not been wiped out.

The other monumental fact of Irish history that makes the Irish different is closely connected with the first. For hundreds of years Ireland was occupied by a foreign power that justified its oppression of another people on the grounds—always implicit and sometimes explicit—that the Irish were an inferior people.

When Michael Collins arrived at Dublin Castle to take charge of it after the ratification of the treaty establishing the Irish free state, he was a bit late.

"You're seven-and-a-half minutes late, General Collins," the British officer snapped with a nasty twist to the word "General."

"You're seven-and-a-half centuries late," Collins responded.

The point was well taken. Seven-and-a-half centuries is a long time for foreign oppression, an oppression that often meant famine, murder, enslavement, persecution, the crushing of every movement for independence, no matter how mild, and the importation of other peoples to replace the bog Irish.

There is a debate now as to whether British rule in Ireland ought to be called genocidal. My feeling is that if the term does not apply to Ireland it does not apply to many places in the world. England set out to destroy the Irish people and almost succeeded. Millions, literally millions, died during the centuries of English misrule—many of them deliberately murdered, others permitted to die by neglect, and still others doomed to starvation in the various famines created by English economic policy. Tens of thousands of women and children were sold into slavery.

Like I say, if that history cannot fairly be called genocide, then the word doesn't have much meaning.

The memory of such suffering does not go away quickly, not even among the American Irish, who now live in an affluence unimagined by royalty not so long ago.

Moreover, a people that survives such murderous oppression acquires or develops character traits (that may already exist in their tradition) that make survival possible. Several research efforts show that the Irish-Americans tend to score high on measures of both fatalism and hope—in fact highest of any American ethnic group. Fatalism and hope, in curious and often paradoxical mixtures, are traits of survivors.

The Irish are also the most likely of any American ethnic group to say that they are "very happy," which should surprise no one who is Irish or knows the Irish. To survive for seven-and-a-half centuries you have to learn to be happy no matter how bad the situation is in which you find yourself.

There is no one more melancholy than a mick who is determined to be melancholy: "They were great times and great people," he will tell you. "Ah, but 'tis all over now. We're the end. It's all finished. They'll not see our like again."

But before the night is finished, and quite possibly with no more of the drink taken, he will sigh and say, "Ah well, I suppose we can't complain. Couldn't it have been worse?"

It is this paradoxical people that I have come to celebrate.

II
Dreamers and Mystics

THE DEER'S CRY

This hymn is also known as "Patrick's Breastplate"

I arise today
Through a mighty strength, the invocation of the Trinity,
Through belief in the threeness,
Through confession of the oneness
Of the Creator of Creation.

I arise today
Through the strength of Christ's birth with His baptism,
Through the strength of His crucifixion with His burial,
Through the strength of His resurrection with His ascension,
Through the strength of His descent for the judgement of Doom.

I arise today
Through the strength of the love of Cherubim,
In obedience of angels,
In the service of archangels,
In hope of resurrection to meet with reward,
In prayers of patriarchs,
In predictions of prophets,
In preaching of apostles,
In faiths of confessors,
In innocence of holy virgins,
In deeds of righteous men.

I arise today
Through the strength of heaven:
Light of sun,
Radiance of moon,
Splendour of fire,
Speed of lightning,
Swiftness of wind,
Depth of sea,
Stability of earth,
Firmness of rock.

I arise today
Through God's strength to pilot me:
God's might to uphold me,
God's wisdom to guide me,
God's eye to look before me,
God's ear to hear me,
God's word to speak for me,
God's hand to guard me,
God's way to lie before me,
God's shield to protect me,
God's host to save me
From snares of devils,

From temptations of vices,
From every one who shall wish me ill,
Afar and anear,
Alone and in a multitude.

I summon today all these powers between me and those evils,
Against every cruel merciless power that may oppose my body and soul,
Against incantations of false prophets,
Against black laws of pagandom,
Against false laws of heretics,
Against craft of idolatry,
Against spells of women and smiths and wizards,
Against every knowledge that corrupts man's body and soul.

Christ to shield me today
Against poison, against burning,
Against drowning, against wounding,
So that there may come to me abundance of reward.
Christ with me, Christ before me, Christ behind me,
Christ in me, Christ beneath me, Christ above me,
Christ on my right, Christ on my left,
Christ when I lie down, Christ when I sit down, Christ when I arise,
Christ in the heart of every man who thinks of me,
Christ in the mouth of every one who speaks of me,
Christ in every eye that sees me,
Christ in every ear that hears me.

I arise today
Through a mighty strength, the invocation of the Trinity,
Through belief in the threeness,
Through confession of the oneness
Of the Creator of Creation.

—Attributed to Saint Patrick,
eighth century

I SHOULD LIKE TO HAVE A GREAT POOL OF ALE

I should like to have a great pool of ale for the King
of Kings; I should like the Heavenly Host to be
drinking it for all eternity.

I should like to have the fruit of Faith, of pure
devotion; I should like to have the couches of
Holiness in my house.

I should like to have the men of Heaven in my own
dwelling; I should like the vats of Long-Suffering
to be at their disposal.

I should like to have the vessels of Charity to dispense;
I should like to have the pitchers of Mercy for
their company.

I should like there to be cheerfulness for their
sake; I should like Jesus to be there too.

I should like to have the Three Marys of glorious
renown; I should like to have the people of
Heaven from every side.

I should like to be vassal to the Lord; if I should
suffer distress He would grant me a good blessing.

*—Attributed to St. Brigid,
tenth century*

ST. COLUMCILLE'S ISLAND HERMITAGE

Delightful I think it to be in the bosom of an isle, on the
peak of a rock, that I might often see there
the calm of the sea.

That I might see its heavy waves over the glittering ocean,
as they chant a melody to their Father on their
eternal course.

That I might see its smooth strand of clear headlands,
no gloomy thing; that I might hear the voice of the
wondrous birds, a joyful course.

That I might hear the sound of the shallow waves against
the rocks; that I might hear the cry by the graveyard,
the noise of the sea.

That I might see its splendid flocks of birds over the
full-watered ocean; that I might see its mighty
whales, greatest of wonders.

That I might see its ebb and its flood-tide in their
flow; that this may be my name, a secret I tell,
"He who turned his back on Ireland."

That contrition of heart should come upon me as I
watch it; that I might bewail my many sins,
difficult to declare.

That I might bless the Lord who has power over all,
Heaven with its pure host of angels, earth, ebb,
flood-tide.

That I might pore on one of my books, good for my
soul; a while kneeling for beloved Heaven, a
while at psalms.

A while gathering dulse from the rock, a while fishing,
a while giving good to the poor,
a while in my cell.

A while meditating upon the Kingdom of Heaven,
holy is the redemption; a while at labour not too
heavy; it would be delightful!

—Attributed to St. Colum,
twelfth century

Only a fool would fail
To praise God in His might
When the tiny mindless birds
Praise Him in their flight

What little throat
Has framed that note
What gold beak shot
It far away

A blackbird on
His leafy throne
Tossed it alone
Across the bay

—Two monastic poems

There's music there
And all kinds of sweetness
In the piper's greeting
At the end of day . . .

—Anonymous

22

SUNLIGHT

There was a sunlit absence.
The helmeted pump in the yard
heated its iron,
water honeyed

in the slung bucket
and the sun stood
like a griddle cooling
against the wall

of each long afternoon.
So, her hands scuffed
over the bakeboard,
the reddening stove

sent its plaque of heat
against her where she stood
in a floury apron
by the window.

Now she dusts the board
with a goose's wing,
now sits, broad-lapped,
with whitened nails

and measling shins:
here is a space
again, the scone rising
to the tick of two clocks.

And here is love
like a tinsmith's scoop
sunk past its gleam
in the meal-bin.

—Seamus Heaney, from "Mossbawn:
Two Poems in Dedication"
(for Mary Heaney)

May you see as clearly as Mary on Christmas morning
As carefully as Joseph on the desert flight
As perceptively as John on the Jordan banks
As bravely as the twelve whom Jesus called
As wildly as the Palm Sunday throng
As sadly as the women 'neath the cross
As gratefully as the forgiven thief
And as joyously as Mary on Easter morn
And may the God of sight make us all to see
Father, Son, and Holy Spirit

May you be as close to God

As the sheep is to the shepherd
As the branch is to the vine
As the flower is to the stem
As the bride is to her groom

As the fish is to the water
As the bird is to the air
As the star is to the sky
As the heat is to the sun

As the plant to its seed
As the leaf to its branch
As the child to her mother
And as God is close to you

And may the God who loves you
Be always with you and bless you
Father, Son, and Holy Spirit

May your faith be strong as a mountain wall
And subtle as the early morning mists
May you believe that God's power conquers all
And his love through trouble and pain persists

May your faith soar like a multicolored bird
And shine brighter than the blinding desert sun
Because you know your prayers are ever heard
And Jesus waits when the final day is done

And may God bless you,
The Father who rules the starry skies
The Son who rose from the dead
And the Spirit who comes in hope

May your hope be as swift as a horse racing by
As deep as the bowels of earth
As high as the star-dense sky
As fresh as a baby's birth

May it be as strong as gravity's force
As resilient as a mother's love
As tenacious as a river's course
As timeless as the gentle Lord above
And may God bless you and renew your hope
Father, Son, and Holy Spirit

May the God of heaven's vault bless you
May the God of shimmering moonlight love you
May the God of sparkling stars lead you
May the God of haunting songs cheer you

May the God of strange shadows calm your nerves
May the God of straight roads bring you home
May God be watching from a familiar window
And hand in hand with Him may you wait for dawn

And may the God of day and night
Bless you, Father, Son, and Holy Spirit

May the God of the misty dawn waken you
May the God of the rising sun stir you up
May the God of morning sky send you on your way
May the God of noonday stillness renew your strength
May the God of afternoon bring you home
May the God of sunset delight your eye
May the God of twilight calm your nerves
And May the God of dusk bring you peace

And may God bless you
The Rising and the Setting Sun
The Alpha and the Omega
The Beginning and the End
Father, Son, and Holy Spirit

May God's strength for you be
As strong as the typhoon wind
As faithful as the daily tide
As sweet as music of the violin
As pervasive as the starry sky

May God's care for you be
As light as a singing thrush
As swift as a mountain stream
As gentle as a baby's touch
As alluring as a lover's gleam

And may God bless you
The Father of power and strength
The Son of wisdom and knowledge
The Spirit of loving care

May you treasure wisely this jeweled, gilded time
And cherish each day as an extra grace
Whose heedless loss would be a tragic crime
In today's tasks may you find God's tender face
May you know that to miss love's smallest chance
Is a lost opportunity, a senseless waste
May you see need in every anxious glance
May you sort out of the dull and commonplace
An invitation to God's merry, manic dance
And May the Lord of the Dance bless you
As he invites you to the dance of the hallowed present
Father, Son, and Holy Spirit

May you see God

In the ice cream cloud
In the wildflower bloom
In the rose light at sunset
In the lover's tender eye

May you hear God

In the fall of raindrops
In the blowing wind
In the singing bird
In the child's gentle cry

May God touch you

In the friendly hand
In new-washed linen
In the mesquite bark
In the lover's kiss

May you smell God

In the rosemary bush
In the orange blossom
In the lover's scent
In the rain-swept sky

May you taste God

In dark chocolate
In raisin buns
In caring lips
And in cherry pie

And may God who lurks everywhere in love

Bless you, Father, Son, and Holy Spirit

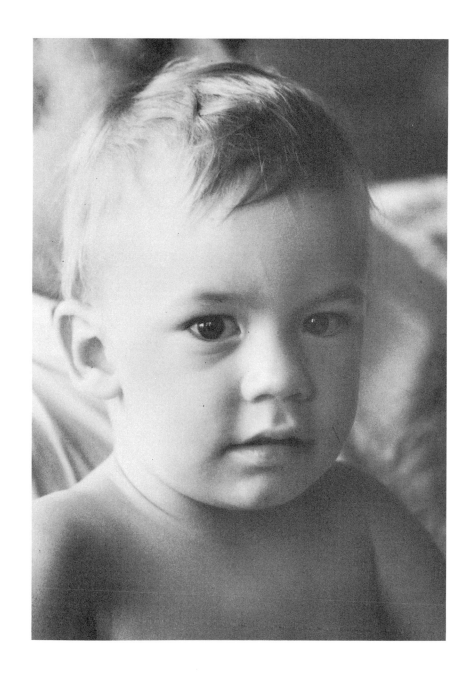

PANGUR BAN

I and Pangur Bán my cat,
'Tis a like task we are at:
Hunting mice is his delight,
Hunting words I sit all night.

Better far than praise of men
'Tis to sit with book and pen;
Pangur bears me no ill will,
He too plies his simple skill.

'Tis a merry thing to see
At our tasks how glad are we,
When at home we sit and find
Entertainment to our mind.

Oftentimes a mouse will stray
In the hero Pangur's way;
Oftentimes my keen thought set
Takes a meaning in its net.

'Gainst the wall he sets his eye
Full and fierce and sharp and sly;
'Gainst the wall of knowledge I
All my little wisdom try.

When a mouse darts from its den
O how glad is Pangur then!
O what gladness do I prove
When I solve the doubts I love!

So in peace our tasks we ply,
Pangur Bán, my cat and I;
In our arts we find our bliss,
I have mine and he has his.

Practice every day has made
Pangur perfect in his trade;
I get wisdom day and night
turning darkness into light.

—*Anonymous, ninth century*

Catholic Christianity slipped into Ireland gently. There were no mass or forced conversions, no bloody battles, no martyrs even till the English came. For a century and a half many folk must have not been too clear whether they were Christian or pagan (like the diminutive heroine, Brigid, in my story, "The Magic Cup"). The gentle and gradual conversion of Ireland to Christianity was surely not complete in the sixteenth century, when the Lords Temporal and Spiritual at the Synod of Maynooth refused to give up their right to have four wives.

Maybe the conversion is not even complete today, though one might argue that the process is much further along than it is in certain other places.

There were two reasons for the gentle and gradual nature of Irish conversion. First, nowhere else in the world did Christianity have enough confidence in itself to take over so completely the symbols of the pagan religion that it encountered than in Ireland. Second, perhaps nowhere else was the pagan religion so easy to assimilate and reinterpret.

I do not want to imply that the pagan Celts were exemplary fellows (and girls) by any means. They were a wild, noisy, roistering, warlike people. They smelled of peat and manure. They also found it very difficult to keep their hands off your women. You wouldn't have wanted them in the neighborhood.

But they and their religion—to which they paid perhaps no more and no less attention than have their descendants—were rather predisposed to the Catholic thinking. Theirs was a sophisticated form of nature religion that did not identify ultimate reality (whatever it might be) with the powers and forces of nature. Rather, the Celts saw the borderline between this world and the other worlds (the many-colored lands, the Land of Promise in the West) as thin and sometimes (at changes of season especially) dangerous thin. The ultimate powers, good and evil, lurked everywhere.

Hence, in their reflective moods the Celts were a mystical and dreamy people, drifting on the borderline between various worlds. One might say that they were a "proto-sacramental" people, already predisposed toward the Catholic theory that God is not absent or distant but hovering everywhere in the persons, events, and objects of ordinary life. It was but a step from pagan dreams to the Christian mysticism of the poetry of the Little Monasteries. One can even draw a direct line from the Celtic poems that see Grace lurking in nature to the contemporary poems of Irish nature mysticism. Look, for example, at the poetry of Seamus Heaney, who sees Grace everywhere, even in his mother baking bread—even, as we shall see later, in an otter swimming in the Desert Museum in Tucson, Arizona.

Mystics and dreamers we may be, but we are not Platonists who reject this world or see it only as a dim mirror of the ultimate reality. The Irish are a people mad with metaphor, but always a metaphor solidly grounded in the poignant, bittersweet, marvelous creation in which we live. Just look at the words that find evidence of God in both the distant world and the concrete reality of the present: "The Deer's Cry," by which St. Patrick is alleged to have disguised himself as a deer while escaping an ambush; the prayer of Brigid for a great pool of ale to celebrate a party for the King of Kings, with hopes Jesus too will be there; Colum's longing for the beauties of his lost Ireland while he lived in exile in Scotland, poor dear man; and above all the greatest of the old poems, the song of Pangur Bán. The cat and the scholar both go about their appointed work, as Mary Heaney does in baking bread. Their response to the God who had made them what they are is to follow that which has been revealed to them. Pangur Bán, perhaps the most famous cat in history, is God's sacrament disclosing how the scholar should live.

As are the blackbird and the great pool of ale and Mrs. Heaney's apron, white with flour.

The thing about an Irish mystic or dreamer is that he can find God almost anywhere and runs the risk of encountering God everywhere.

Sometimes Irish mysticism is equated with an old man sitting by the fire, staring at the burning peat all day long, or leaning on a fence post, pipe in mouth, gazing with glassy eyes out into the bogs.

No doubt there is a certain otherworldliness or, perhaps, a refusal to worry too much that marks these images and Irish mysticism in general. But in recent years, I am sorry to report, this apparent otherworldliness has lacked the paradoxical combination that has always marked Irish mysticism: dreaming and commitment to the work of this world. The friend of Pangur Bán, for instance, did not think he was excused from working. On the contrary, the industry of his cat was a model of industry for him.

Why have we lost that combination? It may be that we Irish-Americans sometimes work too hard and thereby lose some of the peace and reflection, the friendliness and the hospitality of the old Irish countryside.

Or perhaps we have had to work so hard to find a place in this country that we haven't had time for much dreaming. Maybe the heavy drinking that started in Ireland and came with us to this country is an escape from the ugliness imposed upon us which made dreaming and mysticism almost impossible.

Maybe the dreamers will appear in the next generation, dreamers who, like Brigid and Patrick and Colum and Pangur Bán's friend, knew that mysticism and vision were not incompatible with hard work and intense personal responsibility. Maybe that's what the American Irish must be about.

In any case, beware the mick who seems to be staring into the distance. He may be daydreaming, he may be half-asleep, he may be suffering from a hangover.

Or he may be seeing a sacrament like Pangur Bán.

All of which reminds me of the story of Dermot the Eejit. It's a tale whose theme exists in many cultures (in Yiddish, for example, it is the story of the rabbi who went from Kraków to Prague) and is probably a very ancient Indo-European tale.

In the Irish version, however, it is about a peddler. I call him Dermot, and he's the peddler of Ballybogideen.

Now Dermot was a fine young man, if you take my meaning. Weren't his father and mother two of the most hardworking people in the whole parish? And didn't they leave Dermot a snug cottage out in the bogs with a garden for the praties and an orchard of apple trees and a tidy sum of money besides?

And didn't everyone say that Dermot was a fine young man and would do well in life if he wasn't such an eejit?

And why was poor Dermot an eejit?

Well, wasn't he an incorrigible dreamer?

Didn't he take his inheritance and buy himself a peddler's sack because he said that he didn't think he was cut out for farming?

And wasn't he right, the poor dear eejit?

And didn't he let the critters eat all his praties and birds destroy all the fruit on his apple trees?

And when someone suggested that he get a gun and shoot all the critters and all the blackbirds, didn't your man say that he thought he owed them the odd bite to eat because they entertained him so much?

You see what I mean? Your man was a total eejit altogether, wasn't he now?

Like all your eejits, he had no sense at all, at all for business. He'd come into one of the towns near Ballybogideen and spread his wares out in front of the parish church. First thing you know, wouldn't a gosson show up and admire a pocket knife that Dermot was selling? He'd say "Och, Dermot, how much does this grand knife cost?"

"Well," your man would say, cutting the price almost in half, "for you, Seamus, only four shillings, sixpence."

The lad would sigh and hold out his grubby hand and show that he had only two shillings.

"Well, Seamus," your man would say, "there's not a very strong market for pocket knives this season. I think we might let you have it for them two shillings."

And, sure, wouldn't the gosson run home and tell his mother what a wonderful bargain he'd made? And wouldn't the mother say, "Ah, poor Dermot, such a fine boy. Too bad he's a terrible eejit altogether."

Or a colleen would ask to look at his ribbons, and she'd spot a pretty green ribbon that she thought might catch the eye of the fella who had already caught her eye, if you take me meaning. Shy-like, she'd ask Dermot how much it was costing, and he'd tell her sixpence and finally give it to her for twopence because he liked her smile.

Your man was an eejit, wasn't he now?

Well, in the town of Ballybogideen itself, there was a colleen with dark hair and gentle gray eyes and a sweet smile named Sheila. And didn't Dermot catch her eye? And didn't she stand around the crossroads whenever he showed his wares?

But the poor eejit knew he was an eejit and couldn't support a wife and family. So didn't he ignore poor Sheila, who went home one day and cried herself to sleep and never came back to the crossroads?

Well, hard times came to the west of Ireland, and there was not enough food to go around. Everyone knew Dermot would be in trouble, but what could you do with an eejit like him?

Well, one night he was out in his cottage in the bogs with his peddler pack empty and no apples on his trees and no praties in his garden and only one in his house.

Sure, hadn't he tried to sell his cottage and his little patch of land? But in those days, who would spend good money for land out in the bogs?

So there your man was with only a single cold pratie and himself already perishing with the hunger.

So he eats half the pratie and goes to bed without a fire (because he can't afford to buy even a lump of turf).

And who comes to him in a dream but the angel Gabriella herself (from another of my stories)?

"Out of bed with you, Dermot," she says, "and into the town of Ballybogideen. Stand in front of the church and you'll hear what you want to hear and see what you want to see."

Well, your man wakes up in the morning and thinks he's had a foolish dream. Doesn't he go out in the rain and try to find another pratie in his field? But sure the critters hadn't left him a single one.

So that night he eats half of the half of pratie that's left and, sick and cold, he goes to bed.

Doesn't herself come back and, real upset-like, tell him, "Dermot, you eejit. You not only don't have enough sense to come in out of the rain, you don't have enough sense to do what an archangel tells you to do. Out of bed with you, Dermot," she says, "and into the town of Ballybogideen. Stand in front of the church and you'll hear what you want to hear and see what you want to see."

Well, the next morning, doesn't poor Dermot start to walk into the town? But he's so hungry, and the rain is so fierce and the wind so strong that he gives up and walks back to his cottage.

That night he eats the last bit of pratie and says the Act of Contrition because he's not sure how long he'll be living.

Do I have to tell you that herself comes back again, and terrible angry she is? "I want no more Acts of Contrition out of you, Dermot me Bucko. I want you to do what I tell you to do. And first thing in the morning. Or you'll be in terrible trouble altogether. Out of bed with you, Dermot," she says, "and into the town of Ballybogideen. Stand in front of the church and you'll hear what you want to hear and see what you want to see."

So doesn't Dermot, who has a fever now, drag himself out of bed and stumble in the driving rain into the town of Ballybogideen and stand in front of the church all day long?

People walk by him during the day and see him standing in the rain and say to themselves, "Poor Dermot, he's such an eejit. A nice boy, mind you, but he has too many dreams. Now he doesn't even have sense enough to come in out of the rain!"

Well, along about nine o'clock at night the owner of the public house across the street from the church sees Dermot shivering and shaking and soaking wet. He feels sorry for the poor eejit, and he invites him to the pub for a tiny drop and a sandwich or two. Sure, doesn't Dermot accept the invitation and destroy four sandwiches altogether?

The publican likes the young man—sure, didn't everyone like Dermot, and himself being such a terrible eejit—and he gives him a stern little lecture about settling down being the sensible thing to do.

"It's a serious world, lad, and we have to be serious about it. There's no time for dreams and nonsense and such-like, if you take me meaning. It's all hard work and careful planning and determination."

"Yes, sir," says your man, terrible grateful for the food.

"For example, now what were you doing out there all day in the rain?"

"Well, sir," says your man, eejit that he is, not keeping his mouth shut, "didn't the angel Gabriella come to me three nights in a row in a dream and tell me that I should go into the town of Ballybogideen? She said to stand in front of the church and then I'd hear what I wanted to hear and see what I wanted to see."

"Och," says the publican, "aren't you the worst eejit in the whole of creation? I tell you that you can't take dreams seriously. You can't let them interfere with the serious responsibilities of life. Now take me for example. Haven't I been having dreams about an angel too? And doesn't she tell me that there's a cottage somewhere out there in the bogs next to an empty garden and barren apple trees and that beneath the biggest apple tree—between it and the cottage—there's buried treasure? Now a reasonable, sensible man can't pay attention to such nonsense. Buried treasure indeed!" The publican laughed heartily. "I should be leaving me business here and going out into the bogs with a shovel in the pouring rain and dig for buried treasure. Only an amadon would do that."

"Yes, sir," says Dermot meekly.

Now I must be telling you one thing about your man Dermot. He was a terrible eejit, like I've been saying. But he was nobody's fool. So he waits a few minutes, bids a polite good-bye to the publican, thanks him for his sandwiches and pint, and dashes off down the road to the bogs.

He rushes into his house, finds a shovel, and, the rain pouring down, doesn't he start to dig under the largest apple tree?

And he digs and he digs and he digs. Then, just as the sun comes up and stops the rain, doesn't he find a big chest at the bottom of his hole?

Well, doesn't he pull out the chest and pry open the cover and find the buried treasure?

Gold and silver, pieces of eight, pieces of six, stock options, Eurodollars, Ginnie Mae notes, and soybean futures contracts! All kinds of treasure—more money than all the money that had ever been in Ballybogideen put together.

I don't need to tell you who the first one is that hears about the treasure. Sheila, of course, poor dear woman.

And the good the two of them did with all that money—ah, I'd be here all night long and into the morning telling you about that!

III
Talkers and Writers

I go to encounter for the millionth time the reality of experience and to forge in the smithy of my soul the uncreated conscience of my race.

—*James Joyce, from* A Portrait of the Artist as a Young Man, *1916*

ODE

We are the music-makers,
And we are the dreamers of dreams.
Wandering by lone sea-breakers,
And sitting by desolate streams;
World-losers and world-forsakers,
On whom the pale moon gleams:
Yet we are the movers and shakers
Of the world forever, it seems.

With wonderful deathless ditties
We build up the world's great cities,
And out of a fabulous story
We fashion an empire's glory:
One man with a dream, at pleasure,
Shall go forth and conquer a crown;
And three with a new son's measure
Can trample a kingdom down.

We, in the ages lying
In the buried past of the earth,
Built Nineveh with our sighing,
And Babel itself in our mirth;
And o'erthrew them with prophesying
To the old of the new world's worth;
For each age is a dream that is dying,
Or one that is coming to birth.

—*Arthur O'Shaughnessy*

May God protect you
From scary nights
From hasty flights
From too much food
From a somber mood
From ringing bells
From self-made hells
From sickish pains
From dishonest gains
From excessive needs
From tricky deeds
From foolish quarrels
From resting laurels
From silly fears
From idle tears
From forgotten lines
And from all bad times,
Father, Son, and Holy Spirit

May Brigid and Gabriel
Keep your floppy disks unsmashed
And your printer feed unjammed
Your hard disk head uncrashed
And your mind from confusing ROM and RAM

May they remind you
To back up all your text
To know what all your macros mean
And to rest your weary eyes
From the glaring amber screen

May they keep your
Backbone straight, your belly lean
And your dangerous temper mild
Your gentle smile serene
And your patience undefiled

And may God, for whom the world is a PC,
Bless you, Father, Son, and Holy Spirit

(Gabriel is the patron saint of those who work with electronic communications and Brigid the patron saint of poetry and storytelling.)

May you have the strength to push away the sod
And to climb up out of the chilly tomb
May you respond to the trumpet call of God
And explode in life from death's clinging womb
May each day have its own wonder and rebirth
Its molding of new life from unwilling clay
Its springing in surprise from reluctant earth
Its hint of victory on final Judgment Day
And may the God of daily resurrections bless you
Father, Son, and Holy Spirit

May your hand be steady like a canyon rim
And your eye as clear as the desert sky
May your wit and wisdom never turn dim
And your wildest dreams, may they never die
May your laugh be strong when the world seems grim
May fretful, anxious tears all quickly dry
May Jesus watch over you with gentle cherubim
And Mary look down on you with loving eye
And May God bless you and increase your hope
Father, Son, and Holy Ghost

Many years ago in the town of Ballybogideen the parish priest was a very devout and dedicated man named Canon Mulqueen. Some said he was the best parish priest in all of the county Mayo. Others said that he was the best parish priest in the whole west of Ireland—and sure, don't you know that the real Ireland begins only when you cross the river Shannon at Athlone?

But the canon had this one terrible problem, don't you see? Ah, no, it wasn't the drink at all, at all. No, the poor old man was a terrible preacher altogether. He certainly was the worst preacher in the whole of the county Mayo—about that there was no debate. Some said that his homilies were the worst in the whole west of Ireland. A few said that there was no parish priest in the land of Erin who put his congregation to sleep more quickly—and that's covering a lot of territory.

It wasn't so much that his people glanced at their watches every minute or so—they'd be shaking them to see if they had stopped!

Now none of this was because the canon didn't try to prepare his homilies. Ah, no. Sure, didn't the poor man work on them all week long? After the collection was counted on Sunday and locked up and the baptisms entered in the record books, didn't the canon go up to his room and get out his notes and his seminary textbooks and begin working on the homily for next Sunday?

Truth to tell, the more he worked on them, the worse the homilies became!

Well, finally, one Sunday the canon was fed up with it all. He tore up his notes before Mass and walked down the aisle without a sheet of paper in his hand. And weren't some of the congregation noticing that and wondering what was going to happen?

Your man goes through the beginning of Mass like he always has. He puts on his spectacles and reads the Gospel like he always did. He takes off the spectacles and folds them up like he has every Sunday since he first became the parish priest of Ballybogideen.

Then he looks out at the congregation and says, "Sure, aren't you as fine a parish as any in Ireland? And aren't you as bright and intelligent as any congregation of Catholics that exists anywhere in the world? So, there's not a doubt in me mind that you all know what I'm going to preach on in me homily this morning. Now, let me see a show of your hands. How many of you know what I'm about to say?"

No one out there is ready for participated decision making in the Church, so not a hand goes up.

The canon shakes his head in disgust. " 'Tis nothing but a pack of amadons and eejits in church this morning. Well, if you're all too ignorant to know what I'm going to preach about, sure, there's no point in me preaching, is there now?"

And he makes the sign of the cross and goes back to the altar for the rest of Mass.

Well, as you might imagine, there was comment on it in the public houses of the town that week (all five of them). So they were ready for the canon—or so they thought—the next Sunday.

Doesn't he do everything just like before? And when he comes to the homily, doesn't he ask the same question?

"How many of me fine congregation know what I'm going to preach on today?"

And doesn't every hand in the church go up?

"Glory be to God!" shouts your man. "Isn't it a miracle of grace! Well, if you all know what I was intending to say in me homily, sure, there's no point in me saying it. In the name of the Father and of the Son and of the Holy Spirit."

Back he goes to the altar and sails through the rest of Mass like a Galway hooker sailing into port during a storm.

There was, I don't have to tell you, nary a word on any other subject in the public houses all week long. Sure, they all loved and respected the old man, but they were not about to give him any free rides!

So the next Sunday—God forgive them for it, says I—they were loaded for bear when the poor old man closed the Gospel book, put away his spectacles, and peered out at them. He sensed a certain electricity in the air, and—I hate to tell you this—wasn't he loving it?

"Well now," he says, relaxed and casual-like, "I see you're all looking exceptionally bright this morning. Tell me, you've heard me read the Gospel. How many of you would be knowing what I'm going to say in me homily this morning?"

Doesn't everyone on the left-hand side of the church put up his hand?

"Ah, so that's the way of it, is it now?" says your man. "Well, tell me, how many of youse don't know what I'm going to say?"

And doesn't everyone on the right side of the church put up his hand?

"Brigid, Patrick, and Columcille," exclaims the old man, "isn't it another miracle of grace! I tell you what: you on the left side tell the ones on the right side what I was going to say! In the name of the Father and of the Son and of the Holy Spirit."

And doesn't the canon go back to the altar as if he were the captain of the All-Ireland championship football team!

The point about Canon Mulqueen, I guess, is that even though he couldn't talk, he was a great speaker. That is perhaps an Irish bull—a comment that is self-contradictory and yet true. Take these, for example:

"Wasn't it yourself I saw coming down Grafton Street the other day?"

"Ah, 'twas not."

"I didn't think so. By the time I caught up with you you were gone."

Or, take this comment from a woman standing in line to get on a bus: "Sure, if all of us get on, there won't be room for the half of us."

No matter how you explain it—genes or culture or a mixture of both—the Irish have not so much a gift with words as a passion for them. The real Irish produce more novelists, poets, storytellers, and playwrights per capita than any other country in the world. And you could make a case that the best novelist, playwright, and poet in the English language in the twentieth century all came from Ireland.

They've never stopped talking, of course. But I'm told by those who know more about such things than I do that modern languages have smaller conversational vocabularies than do archaic languages. For some reason there is movement toward simplification as languages evolve. Tenses, declensions, conjugations all tend to disappear, and while the dictionaries become thicker, the ordinary vocabulary that people use in everyday conversations becomes smaller. Thus the typical English-speaking person has four thousand words comprising most of his conversational vocabulary.

The Irish-speaking folk in the west of Ireland use six thousand words in their common vocabulary. And the conversational vocabulary of the English speakers in Ireland increases in size as their locale approaches the Irish-speaking fringes.

Rich languages seem to be a casualty of universal literacy, modernization, and education. And a serious loss it is. Whether it is a necessary loss I don't know—though the number of books available to improve one's vocabulary suggests that many of us are at least dimly aware of the loss.

It may be, then, that the Irish passion for words is another example of the survival of an archaic trait in the modern world. Will the trait continue to endure as Ireland becomes part of the highly rationalized (and very dull) European community? Is the romance with words dying out?

Anyone who has visited Ireland and listened to ordinary conversation knows that the love affair does not seem to be growing cold.

The Irish-Americans, of course, are also given to scribbling and talking and, in recent years, seem to be making up for lost time in the production of novels and short stories. And no one has suggested that Irish-Americans are a silent bunch. Not at all, at all.

In my novel *Nell Pat*, Dermot Michael Quinn, a young American living in

Dublin, is "chatting up" a "druid goddess" from Trinity College in O'Neill's pub on Suffolk Street. He admits ruefully that he is not very good at anything. He flunked out of Notre Dame, failed to graduate from Marquette, quit the football team in high school. No, he says, he's not good at anything, not at all, at all.

"Except talking," Nuala McGriel tells him. "Except talking."

Well, naturally.

Still, we Irish-Americans are not as passionate about words because we are part of a society that misuses words all the time, draining them of meaning because of overuse and abuse. Yet we disproportionately choose careers in fields that require skill with words—law, journalism, English literature, writing. Moreover, our young people are more likely to take courses in Irish history and literature and thus open up the channels to the source of the Irish passion for words. People like my colleague Charles Fanning are doing serious studies of Irish-American literature. Perhaps someday there will be courses in that subject at University College, Dublin, or even at Trinity.

May we Irish-Americans never become quiet and reserved, dignified and solemn. May the words continue to flow.

Research data show that, so far, the words have continued to flow: Irish-American adults on the average talk several more hours a week with their spouses and children than do other Americans. But, as one Irish-American (male) said to me, "You measured only talk, not listening to what the other says."

"That's not part of the rules of the game," I replied. "Who ever said 'listen'?"

For many of us the only audience we really need is our best audience—ourselves. An addition of others is welcome but unessential.

On the other hand, the Irish also have a gift of saying nothing at all when the situation is appropriate. Take, for instance, the politician who never answered with a sentence when he could respond with a word, never answered with a word when he could answer with a grunt, never answered with a grunt when he could respond with a shrug of his shoulders, and never shrugged his shoulders when he could get away without answering at all.

Sometimes silence is the most powerful and ingenious form of speech.

The Irish, as I've noted, score high on measures of happiness and hope, both in this country and in Ireland. I believe their scores reflect both the passion for words I've talked about here and the nature mysticism I described in the preceding chapter. Put together an ancient ability to see creation as sacramental, revelatory, and an equally ancient skill for using language to describe the mystery of the ordinary, and you have the raw material for a reasonably happy life.

Moreover, the Irish "stories of God" both in this country and in Ireland are benign. The Irish are the most likely to score high on images of God as lover, friend, spouse, and mother and to score low on images of God as judge, king, master, and father. These images of a loving relationship with God naturally shape Irish response to human social reality and make the Irish, despite self-hatred and anti-Irish bigotry, a tolerant people. Irish-Americans, in fact, may be the most liberal and tolerant gentile ethnic group in this country. To experience ultimate reality as benign—and to be able to give voice to that experience—makes for a more gracious and happy life.

It is not a bad thing to be Irish.

IV
Lovers and Friends

Two shorten the road.

No, I don't know your age, Macushla,
but whatever it is, you sure don't look it.

People live in one another's shelter.

A friend's eye is a good mirror.

—Irish proverbs

"Oh my grief, I've lost him surely. I've lost the only
playboy of the Western World."

—John M. Synge, from The Playboy of
the Western World, *1907*

'Down with marriage! It's out of date;
It exhausts the stock and cripples the state.
The priest has failed with whip and blinker,
Now give a chance to Tom the Tinker,
And mix and mash in Nature's can
The tinker and the gentleman!
Let lovers in every lane extended
Struggle and strain as God intended
And locked in frenzy bring to birth
The morning glory of the earth;
The starry litter, girl and boy
Who'll see the world once more with joy.
Clouds will break and skies will brighten,
Mountains bloom and spirits lighten,
And men and women praise your might,
You who restore the old delight.'

—Brian Merriman, from
"The Midnight Court,"
eighteenth century

THE OTTER

When you plunged
The light of Tuscany wavered
And swung through the pool
From top to bottom.

I loved your wet head and smashing crawl,
Your fine swimmer's back and shoulders
Surfacing and surfacing again
This year and every year since.

I sat dry-throated on the warm stones.
You were beyond me.
The mellowed clarities, the grape-deep air
Thinned and disappointed.

Thank God for the slow loadening,
When I hold you now
We are close and deep
As the atmosphere on water.

My two hands are plumbed water.
You are my palpable, lithe
Otter of memory
In the pool of the moment,

Turning to swim on your back,
Each silent, thigh-shaking kick
Re-tilting the light,
Heaving the cool at your neck.

And suddenly you're out,
Back again, intent as ever,
Heavy and frisky in your freshened pelt,
Printing the stones.

—*Seamus Heaney*

May Brigid and Patrick bring joy to your heart
And the singing and dancing on this golden night
May you and all your true loves never part
And your path ahead be always bright
For now wisdom and grace and fun only start
And hope reaches forth to the coming of light
May you protect others from the scary dark
And see God's endless love make all things right

And May God bless you and grant you fifty more
Father, Son, and Holy Spirit

May Jesus and Mary guide you on your way
Through all of life's stops and starts
May the promise of this wedding day
Be kept alive in both your hearts

May the rhythms of daily life
Give new strength to your love and faith
May you triumph over foolish strife
And come home together sound and safe

May troubles give you in their turn
A challenge to begin again
May you with hope and joy thus learn
Surely that love need never end

May the God of passionate love bless you
Father, Son, and Holy Spirit

May God skim waves with you in years ahead
And charge with you against offensive lines
May you be healthy and happy and ever well fed
And watch TV at all appropriate times

May Mother Mary keep you close in love
So you love each other as her Son loves you
Till your lives continue in heaven above
And in eternity you're to each other true

May you welcome your guests with cheerful glee
And sing and tell stories with them all night long
May in one another you the Lord Jesus see
So that where you are He also belongs

May the God of love keep you always close
Father, Son, and Holy Ghost

May leaves of autumn decorate your path
May mellow golden sunlight guide your way
May love and laughter overcome all wrath
And renew the joy of your wedding day
May October warmth turn away the cold
And Indian summer haze soothe life's pain
May God protect your romance from growing old
And, if it wilts, refresh your love again

And may God bless you and keep you always
The Father who creates love
The Son who renews it
And the Holy Spirit who guards us from the cold

As warm bread is sliced by a gleaming knife
May sunlight cut through the harsh winter cold
May God's love shine brightly in your common life
And may your own romance be never old
May hope increase with each lengthening day
And rout the ache of hurt and conflict's gloom
May loyal friends never be far away
With the promise that spring will surely bloom
May our good God of songs round the fireplace
Of love and laughter, of good wine and fun
Lurk always in your home's hidden space
And bind you in love when each day is done

And may God bless you and keep you close
Father, Son, and Holy Spirit

May a silver moon reign over this harvest night
And glorious Irish dreams explode anew
May those glittering blue eyes dance with light
While argent stars whirl to the pipes with you
May your journey be at least twice as long
And your kids prevent you from growing old
May Jesus and Mary join in your song
And henceforth may every day be purest gold

And may the Lord of the Great Sacrament
Bless you, Father, Son, and Holy Spirit

May your pilgrimage to the rainbow-colored lands
Go joyous on a glowing yellow-brick way
By a gentle sea, across the glittering sands
Wrapped in the friendly warmth of middle day
May you realize that God's golden light
Which oft urges you to quickly hasten on
And escape the frightening shades of night
Is not fading sunset but exploding dawn
And may God bless you
The Father who created you
The Son who showed you God's goodness
And the Holy Spirit who
Binds you, like Them, in love

May Jesus bless and bind your love today
May Mary keep your pledge alive and strong
May spring flowers bright always mark your way
And blue skies shelter a journey safe and long
May conflict never take your peace away
May good friends protect you from every wrong
May you answer always God's call to play
And your eyes sparkle with laughter, joy, and song
And may the God who changed water into wine
Bless and protect your life together
Father, Son, and Holy Spirit

May Jesus and Mary make straight your road
May blue skies shine on all your parades
May your years stretch on to silver and gold
May your love be the sort that never fades

For every winter may there come a spring
For every hurt a quick and healing hand
For every doubt the hope that's in this ring
For every fear the promise in this magic band

May God bless you
The Father who created love
The Son who came in love
And the Spirit who keeps love alive

May Jesus and Mary be at your side
As close to you as your wedding rings
Where you are may they abide
And angels shade you 'neath their wings

May the quick, warm winds of spring
Sweep away all grimy clouds
Joy and happiness ever bring
And exorcise any deadly doubts

May your love be never ending
And may you one another guide
Onward from this happy wedding
And from each other never hide

Two lovers in whatever crowd
To each other may you always cling
Of your hope and laughter proud
In good and bad and everything

May Jesus who came to Cana and
His mother who saved the party
Protect you always
And may He bless you together
With the Father and the Holy Spirit

May your love be blessed by Valentine
And renewed by the God who loves us all
May sweet nothings your lover bind
And dark chocolate early love recall

May valentine lace revive the past
And your own romance, once more on fire,
In its passion experienced again at last
Reveal God present in your ardent desire

And may the God who created
Out of passionate love
Rekindle all your loves
So that you may know God better
Father, Son, and Holy Spirit

May your parades be drenched by the cheerful sun
May your loves be smiled on by the friendly moon
May Jesus wait for you when life is done
And may Mary grant that it not be soon
May the wind brush softly against your face
May the daisies and daffodils line your way
May you be bathed by God's bounteous grace
And enjoy all the gifts for which you pray
And may you be blessed by the God
Who calls us all friends
Father, Son, and Holy Spirit

May the Spirit's warmth renew the love of your life
May God's strength help you to be brave
In tenderness, not weak in petty strife
May God's wisdom your sensitivity save
When frustration and discontent are rife
So that gently passion's bond be remade
May your delicacy be keen as a knife
And your gentle persistence never fade
Till love's old romance is at last remade
And may the God of Love bless you and
Bind you together as He binds the universe
With the attraction of gravity's power
Father, Son, and Holy Spirit

May the Lord God be with us at this meal
And bless us and the food we're about to eat
May this table our love and friendship seal
As we give thanks for our bread and wine and meat
May we be gracious to those who come in need
And to the lonely ones we perhaps can heal
In those who want, the Lord's holy presence heed
And gratitude to our cook most profoundly feel

The blessing of the five loaves and two fishes
That God shared among the five thousand,
The bounty of the King made the sharing,
Come upon our food and all who share it.

May God give you to drink from the well that never runs dry.

A hundred glories to you, bright God of heaven,
Who gave us this food and the sense to eat it
Give mercy and glory to our souls
And life without sin to ourselves and to the poor.

Praise to the King who is not miserly
Praise at all times to God.
Praise and thanksgiving to Jesus Christ for the food we have eaten.

May He who gave us this food
Give us also the food of everlasting life.

—Meal prayers from the Irish language

The rabbi and the priest had become good friends during their trip together in Ireland. One afternoon they had a good warm lunch in a pub in the west of Ireland and a drop or two of the drink. Then they went for a walk in the sunlight down one of the back lanes and had themselves a very intimate and personal conversation.

"Now, Rabbi," says the priest, " 'tis clear to me that you are a holy and devout man, what with all them terrible dietary laws you have to keep. Sure, I couldn't keep them to save my life. But tell me, man to man now, you don't keep them all all the time, do you? I mean, for example, have you ever in all your life eaten ham?"

"That's a very personal question, Father." The rabbi looked around anxiously to see if there was anyone lurking in the hedgerows who might hear the conversation.

"I won't tell a soul, Rabbi. Seal of confession."

"Seal of confession?"

"Seal of confession."

"Well, once, when I was in college and eaten up with curiosity, yes, I'll admit it, I ate a ham sandwich."

"You're an honest man to admit it, Rabbi," says the priest. "Sure, 'twas no more than a venial sin."

That was back in the days when we had venial sins.

"Ah, Father," says the rabbi, "fair is fair now. Let me ask you a personal question. Have you ever slept with a woman?"

"That's a terrible question!" the priest shouts at him.

"Seal of confession, Father!"

"You won't tell my bishop?"

"Seal of confession!"

"Well . . ." The priest looks around anxious-like to make sure no one can hear him. "Fair is fair, I guess. I'll admit it. Once, when I was in college, the blood was hot, and I was on fire with curiosity, so, yes, I did spend a night in bed with a woman."

"Beats ham, doesn't it?"

Like all the rabbi/priest jokes, this one shows the rabbi as triumphant, so it's pretty clear which ethnic group starts them.

There is a hint in the joke, however, of a stereotype of the Irish that often seems even to the Irish to be partially true: a view of the Irish as sexually cold and rigid, as a puritanical people who do not enjoy intimacy of any kind. It's an ironic stereotype, when you stop to think it was Cromwell and his Puritans who did much to destroy ancient Irish civilization, which was anything but "puritanical." Before Puritan thought came to Ireland, eroticism had been condoned and encouraged as a natural and beautiful part of life—and had received the blessing of the Catholic Church.

Trial marriage (which husband or wife could end after a year and a day) had been a tradition from the pre-Christian Brehon laws, which continued well into the Christian era. Premarital sexual amusements were also part of the tradition, as Brian Merriman's famous poem "The Midnight Court" proves—though there was also a Celtic tradition of chastity that was fiercely practiced by the Irish women long before Christianity. Whenever there was a reasonable amount of food available and the crops were good, young men and women married young and showed no signs of being ashamed of their sexual joys.

Although Irish monasticism was often fiercely penitential, the Irish who did not become monks were not a sexually inhibited people for the first millennium of their history. Indeed, not all the monks were so penitent. Many of the abbots willed their monasteries to their sons.

Nor was the Irish church opposed to sexual pleasure, either officially or unofficially. Indeed, at the Synod of Maynooth (site of the present national seminary) in 1540 one of the items on the agenda was a law outlawing concubinage, the ancient Brehon law permitting the nobility to have four wives. The law was never voted on, however, because most of the lords present, spiritual as well as temporal, were practicing the custom.

It is not my intent to defend either trial marriages or polygamy but only to say that Puritanism was an English disease at first, not an Irish one. Puritanism was an English import and its Catholic cousin, Jansenism, an import from

France, where Irish young men went to study for the priesthood during penal times.

So was it only Puritanism that led to sexual repression in Ireland? No, 'twas the Great Famine that added fuel to the fire. The Famine, of course, created great financial hardship, and the Irish began to delay marriage so they could control the growth of their population and assure the orderly passage of the family farm from father to son. The Church, after years of blessing early marriages and large families during pre-Famine prosperity, opposed these new trends—yet still insisted on premarital chastity. What were young men and women to do whose families wanted later marriages? Well, let us just note that the old erotic traditions of trial marriages and lots of carrying-on went underground, never to disappear entirely. In fact, these traditions seem to be resurfacing in Ireland today.

And what about the Irish-Americans?

Well, their rate of sexual intercourse is the highest of any ethnic group in the country—though one does not have to believe that they're telling the truth. The younger generation has made up its mind that the pope, poor dear man, does not understand how important sexual love is in healing the pain and the friction of the common life. Most of the clergy—in both Ireland and America—seem to agree with them. The Puritan phase in Irish culture is over. A return to the more ancient heritage, never completely eradicated, seems to be taking place.

So now it's all right again for men to admit they find women desirable and for women to admit they find men desirable.

It is all right to admit that our species is designed to fall repeatedly in love, one hopes with the same person.

It is all right for priests to admit that they find women attractive and that they have erotic fantasies about them. It is all right for priests to admit that they too fall in love, hopefully keeping their vows.

It is all right even for priests to take pictures of beautiful women, as long as the pictures respect the women.

The sexual energies that drive our species are such that no one can ever be confident that those energies are in control over the long run. But the answer to the imperious power of sexuality is not to deny that it exists (as the Puritans tried to do and as the Vatican often seems to want Catholics to do), because repression never works. Rather the answer is to live cautiously and prudently with this delightful and overwhelming drive.

The Catholic sacramental tradition, which is, as I have argued, especially compatible with Irish culture, must rejoice in this change. There is more Catholic awareness of the sacramentality of sex—its power to reveal the passion of God's love for us—in the poetry of Brian Merriman and Seamus Heaney (alone in Tucson and fantasizing about his wife as he watches an otter swim in a pool at the Desert Museum) than there is in the repressive sexual "rules" many of us were taught in school or catechism classes or on retreats.

If Catholicism is to rediscover—or discover for the first time, perhaps—the power of the sexual image as a sacrament of God's love, the Irish, with their ancient erotic tradition and their insight, often preconscious, that sex defies death, ought to be taking the lead.

I think that's already happening with novelists like Maeve Binchy (especially in her wonderful book *Echoes*) and poets like Seamus Heaney.

It is to the poets and the storytellers that one must look for such imagery—and not to the theologians.

Perhaps we must also look to the photographers and the artists who know that there is no human face that does not somehow reflect God's glory (especially when the face is upturned in prayer), no human form that somehow does not invite God's love, and no age in life in which humans are not capable of intimacy (of one sort or another). And that intimacy has the possibility of being a radical sign of the presence of God.

As Monsignor John B. "Blackie" Ryan (a character in my novels) puts it, "Sexuality is one of the trickiest games Lady Wisdom plays with us to reveal what She's really like."

Haven't the Irish known that all along?

The poets knew it anyway, even if some of the priests and all of the bishops didn't.

As a final note, I might add that in *The Irish Comic Tradition*, the late Vivian Mercer shows how that tradition has been shaped by an often grotesque eroticism that shows life stronger than death. One example of this eroticism is the ancient Irish custom of making love in the fields around a house where a corpse lay. The custom is rooted in pre-Christian days and survived as part of the Christian wake into the nineteenth century. In effect the custom became a traditional way of saying, "Screw you, Death. Life is stronger than you!"

Which reminds me of a true story about friends of mine whom I had known in Chicago. The wife, a real Irish, and her husband, an Irish-American, were once visiting Ireland, and while there they decided to try to resuscitate this custom by conceiving their first child in a potato field (at night, mind you). They were successful in their efforts, thanks be to God, and the resulting boy child was promptly nicknamed Spuds.

Spuds and his parents soon moved far from my Chicago home, and I had occasion to see them only now and then. On one of their early visits I asked how they would explain the nickname to Spuds when he grew old enough to ask the question.

Sufficient to the evil, they said, is the day thereof.

Well, I saw them again when Spuds was fourteen.

"Ask your question, Father Greeley," says herself.

"Spuds," says I, "why do they call you Spuds?"

"Because, Father Greeley," he replies, his face beaming with pride, "I was conceived in a potato field in Ireland."

Good enough for the priest! That put him in his place!

V
Celebrants and Disputants

Confusion to our enemies and God's choicest blessings on all our friends.

You don't have to be a peace-seeker to be happy in Ireland, but if you are you will find what you seek.

—Conor Cruise O'Brien,
twentieth century

May God grant that my friends continue to be my friends
May God grant that the hearts of my enemies be turned so that they become my friends
And if He cannot turn their hearts, would He please turn their ankles so I know them by their walk!

When Irish eyes are smiling
All the world is bright and gay.

—Popular song

May you be with goodness profligate
As winter is with flakes of snow
As fall with leaves of red and gold
To all, if early come, or late
And your friends' needs anticipate

When sagging spirits bring them low
May you warm them with your loving glow
As winter sun bathes a frozen lake
And may you be blessed
By the Father of profligate creation
The Son of superabundant wisdom
And the Spirit of exuberant love

May your hope be

As determined as the river racing by
As soft as the cry of the mourning dove
As sweet and subtle as a lover's sigh
As glorious as reborn human love

As resolute as the sun rising each day
As certain as the return each year of spring
May it break through the darkling clouds
And confirm you against every evil thing

May Jesus and Mary and Patrick and Brigid
Strengthen your faith and hope and love

And may God bless you
Father, Son, and Holy Spirit

May Jesus and Mary and Patrick
Grant you happiness and joy
Festivity, celebration, and also fun
Broad hints of glee without alloy
When at last our work is done

The joy of Easter morn
The joy of Christmas night
The joy of a new baby born
The joy of all delights

The joy of a graduation class
The joy of delicious food
The joy of a wedding Mass
The joy of old love renewed

And may Jesus who came to bring us joy
Bless you always, together with
The Father and the Holy Spirit

TIM FINNEGAN'S WAKE

Tim Finnegan lived in Walkin' Street,
A gentle Irishman mighty odd,
He'd a beautiful brogue so rich and sweet
and to rise in the world he carried a hod.
You see he'd a sort o' the tipplin' way,
with a love for the liquor poor Tim was born,
to help him on with his work each day,
He'd a drop o' the cray-thur every morn.

Chorus

Whack fol the da now,
Dance to your partner
welt the floor
your trotter's shake
wasn't it the truth I told you
Lots of fun at Finnegan's wake

One morning Tim was rather full,
His head felt heavy, which made him shake,
He fell from a ladder, and he broke his skull,
and they carried him home his corpse to wake.
They rolled him up in a nice clean sheet
And laid him out upon the bed,
With a gallon of whiskey at his feet,
And a barrel of porter at his head.

Chorus

His friends assembled at the wake
And Mrs. Finnegan called for lunch
First they brought in tay, and cake,
Then pipes, tobacco, and whiskey punch.
Biddy O'Brien began to cry,
Such a nice clean corpse did you ever see?
Tim Mavoureen, why did you die?
Arrah hold your gob, said Paddy McGhee.

Chorus

Then Maggie O'Connor took up the job,
Oh Biddy, says she, you're wrong I'm sure
Biddy gave her a belt in the gob,
And left her sprawling on the floor.
Then the war did soon engage,
'Twas woman to woman, and man to man,
Shillelagh law was all the rage,
and a row and a ruction soon began.

Chorus

Then Mickey Maloney raised his head,
When a noggin of whiskey flew at him.
It missed and, falling on the bed,
The liquor scattered over Tim.
Tim revives—see how he rises—
Timothy rising from the bed,
Said, "Whirl your whiskey around like blazes,
Thanum an dial, do you think I'm dead?"

Chorus

—Old Irish ballad

REILLY'S DAUGHTER

As I was sitting by the fire,
talking to old Reilly's daughter,
suddenly a thought came into my head,
I'd like to marry old Reilly's daughter.

Giddy I ae for the one-eyed Reilly,
giddy I ae,
(bang, bang, bang)
Try it on your own big drum

Reilly played on the big bass drum,
Reilly had a mind for murder and slaughter,
Reilly had a bright red, glittering eye,
And he kept that eye on his lovely daughter.

Her hair was black and her eyes were blue,
The colonel and the major and the captain sought her,
The sergeant and the private and the drummer boy too,
But they never had a chance with Reilly's daughter.

I got me a ring and a parson too,
Got me a scratch in a married quarter,
Settled me down to a peaceful life,
Happy as a king with Reilly's daughter.

Suddenly a footstep on the stairs,
Who should it be but Reilly out for slaughter
With two pistols in his hands,
Looking for the man who had married his daughter.

I caught old Reilly by the hair,
Rammed his head in a pail of water,
Fired his pistols into the air,
A damned sight quicker than I married his daughter.

—*Old Irish song*

I must be perfectly honest about one failure of mine to live up to the Irish tradition.

I go to bed early—usually between ten and eleven o'clock. I admit with a shamed face that such a practice is a violation of my Irish heritage, especially my Irish clerical heritage.

My sister, like me in most respects, is totally different on this key item. She and her husband and their kids are always the last ones to go home from a party—and usually make a stop somewhere else to continue the celebration. But I always bail out early, my departure hardly noticed because no one expects me to be around for the "best part" of a celebration. I do this even if the party happens to be in my honor.

I can't explain this aberration. And I know what my penance may be in purgatory: I'll have to stay up all night to make up for all the parties out of which I have pooped.

These parties from which I disappear early are not drunken brawls. I admit that the Irish have been known to have such, particularly on St. Patrick's Day— the celebration of which is, in this country, a disgrace to the Irish heritage and to the holy saint. The Irish parties I attend are more often reasonably sober, remarkably sober by American standards. Becoming drunk spoils much of the fun of a party. The real fun, you see, is to be found in eating and talking, singing and dancing, talking and laughing, and, of course, arguing.

Celebrating and disputing are not necessarily incompatible activities. For the Irish I know, they are not only compatible; they are correlates. You celebrate so you can argue, you argue so you can celebrate—and then dance and sing some more.

Meanwhile I'm home in bed getting a good night's sleep.

As I've hinted several times in this book, I am offended by the Irish drinking stereotype and even more by the efforts of some of my fellow Irish-Americans to prove the stereotype correct. The real Irish are in the bottom third of the European community countries in per-capita alcohol consumption, and I've already mentioned similar statistics for the American Irish. The "drunken mick" image, as sociologist Richard Stivers has pointed out in a brilliant book, appropriately titled *The Hair of the Dog*, is a negative stereotype imposed on an immigrant people by those who hated them. As often happens in such cases of powerful and vicious stereotyping, the victim group tried to turn the image around and make it a happy stereotype; the Irish immigrants and their children converted the image from that of a brutal drunk to that of a happy drunk, a celebrating instead of a disputing drunk. However, as in any such conversion process, the stereotype is accepted and internalized. Instead of being ashamed of their reputation as big drinkers, many Irish-Americans became proud of it.

I am not a prohibitionist. I do not object to the drink being taken, not as long as the one doing the taking is not driving a car. The "creature," as the Irish term the drink, is a grand lubricant for celebrating and disputing.

Rather I object to the impact of this inverted stereotype on Irish-American family life. I object to the need that many Irish seem to feel to outdrink everyone else—as though this were a great achievement. I object to the myth that the Irish cannot have a good celebration or a good argument if they're sober. I object to the image that the Irish wake is always a drunken brawl.

Those objections are not the reasons I poop out at parties. I don't even go to the ones that I think are going to end up as brawls. I go home because I'm tired, because my physiology, perhaps in the form of a mutant gene, makes it impossible for me to think straight after 11:30 and to keep my eyes open after midnight.

The point here is that the Irish can and do have fun and can and do engage in great and wondrous arguments stone sober. Not all of them do it, but some do and more should. The drunkenness in the Irish tradition has a long history, back to pagan times. However, the current manifestations of it as an extreme problem seem to have originated in the post-Famine depression and frustration and gloom—one more blessing of English imperialism.

But the sobriety tradition, the tradition of great fun without too much of the drink taken, is equally ancient and much more honorable. We Irish would do everyone a great service, especially ourselves, if we shared in it more with others.

The annual Emerald Ball of Old Saint Patrick's parish in Chicago (at which some of these Irish faces were captured) is the best Irish party of the year, and almost no one drinks too much—though what happens after eleven o'clock I report on the basis of the testimony of others and not as a result of personal observation.

The Dublin ballad "Tim Finnegan's Wake" is certainly a lively song, particularly when the Clancy Brothers belt it out (and some of them Pioneers, those liquid celibates, at that). Moreover, it has been forever immortalized in your man's great novel (which I contend is part put-on). Nor would I deny for a moment that such wakes have occurred in Ireland and in Irish America—though I've never been to one and I am convinced that the drunken brawl wakes are an exception.

In Ireland the Church pretty much succeeded in its millennium-and-a-half campaign against wakes—as it did in eliminating the other two abuses it thought it saw in Irish piety: holy wells and "patterns," which are festivals at the shrines of saints on their feast days. However, having rehabilitated and reinterpreted both the holy wells and the pattern (in the finest tradition of Irish Catholicism's historic commitment to taking over and "baptizing" paganism), the Irish church is beginning to wonder if something can't be done about reviving the wake. Some Irish liturgists and theologians are beginning to note that the idea of laughing at death, purified of the abuse of alcohol, might not be a bad one at all.

As for the lovemaking in the fields mentioned earlier—ah, well, what people do after a wake is their business now, isn't it, especially if they are married? I cannot think of a more appropriate response to death than passionate love. Mind you, I'll say nothing about how lovemaking is done in potato fields. I don't know how you do that, and I don't want to know!

Regardless of that ancient custom, the Irish-American wakes I've attended are not at all like Tim Finnegan's wake. Rather they are much more like Knocko

Minnehan's wake in Edwin O'Connor's *The Last Hurrah*, especially as it was portrayed in the wondrous Spencer Tracy film version.

The typical Irish-American wake that I know is relatively quiet and not without its element of sadness. On the average, however, such wakes are devoid of hysteria and despair. They are, to describe them precisely, celebrations of a faith (older than Christianity but strongly reinforced by Christianity) that life is stronger than death. A celebratory people, the Irish do *not* celebrate death; rather they celebrate their conviction that life triumphs over death.

Some Irish-Americans are ashamed of the wake custom and ease it out of their family traditions—a rejection that is surely their privilege. The Irish way of death is different, and no one is under any obligation to sustain that difference—or any other. However, I think that in the kind of wake I have described one finds the reason why the Irish are a celebratory people: they have believed in human survival for a long time—longer even than they have been Christian. Much of the Irish and Irish-American character—the dreaming, the mysticism, the talking, the writing, the loving, the arguing, the celebrating—can be explained by this conviction.

If you want to understand the faces around which this book is structured, you must realize that, in some cases perhaps against their propositional convictions, these folk believe in the triumph of life.

It used to be frequently argued that the "supernaturalism" of the Irish religion is responsible for the poverty of the Irish in Ireland and the lack of achievement of the Irish in America. It is religion, you see, and not three-quarters of a millennium of oppression by a genocidal foreign power, that is the cause of the Irish problem. The countrymen in the west of Ireland, you understand, lack the ambition necessary to improve their condition in life because their religion promises them life after death, pie in the sky when they die.

If only they weren't so Catholic, the Irish would be all right.

The bigotry of that argument is not sufficiently evident that you don't still hear it on occasion, even in respectable social science circles.

The enormous success of Irish-Catholic Americans destroys the argument completely, but only if you are willing to believe the data about that success; and not everyone, not even some Irish-Americans, are willing to believe those statistics.

In fact, from pre-Christian time, the Irish belief in the Land of Promise in the West did not interfere with concern about and commitment to the problems and possibilities of this world. Irish poverty was not and is not the result of "otherworldliness" but of oppression. The Irish countryman was not kept from achievement by his religion but by the occupying power and its landlords—who also did their best to deprive him of his religion. As soon as he or his children escaped the oppression, they began to do very well indeed. By 1900, for example, Irish-Catholic Americans were more likely to attend college than average white Americans.

The present land, the world in which we live, is a sacrament of the Land of Promise in the West, not an impediment to it.

The conviction that life is victorious over death is surely worth celebrating— even to the wee hours.

Only don't expect me to be present for the end of the party.

VI
Women and Kids

Praise the young and they will blossom.

A raggy colt often made a powerful horse.

Women do not drink liquor but it disappears when they are present.

It is a lonely washing that has no (man's) shirt in it.

If you want to be criticized, marry.

You must live with a person to know a person.

Your feet will bring you to where your heart is.

There is no fireside like your own fireside.

Men are like bagpipes: no sound comes from them until they are full.

From the day you marry your heart will be in your mouth
and your hand in your pocket.

—Irish proverbs

My love lives in a distant valley,
and it's the sweetest of all places,
Every treetop bends down with berries and
every blossom spreads round its fragrance.
Oh, if my darling and I were married and our
good fortune did not fail us,
The golden sovereigns in our pockets would
pay the lady of the alehouse.

But the sunshine is drowned in darkness, the
light of stars and moon is waning,
And the pathways I cannot master, for my own
eyesight is surely fading.
With bitter tears for that sweet lady whose kiss
of honey I've never tasted;
And, Oh my darling, relieve my hardship, for
it's your charms that have me wasted.

So I will quit now this bitter townland, for it
has left me sick and broken,
And I'll go seeking my only sweetheart in every
place where her name is spoken.
Oh, the teardrops they have me blinded, the
clearest signpost I cannot follow,
And it's my heartache I will not wake where
you lay your dark hair on your pillow.

—*Irish poem*

DELVACHEEM

Symbol of God, are you, girl, saving grace
Her warmth in your fair breast's inviting glow?
Fire and ice, revealed in your soft embrace
Black hair on white shoulders, lava on the snow?
Does She arouse, inflame with timid eye,
Respond, pliant, meek to our hungry need?
Give Herself in love with complacent sigh
Seek our pleasure with single-minded greed?

Then ravished does She turn us fugitive
Hunting with now enraptured charms?
Caught by Her, wildly, madly, pinned captive
Imprisoned in forever-loving arms
Thus Her feather touch sets our hearts awhirl
'Tis You we see in the body of this girl.

—A. G.

PRAYER FOR AN IRISH MODEL

"Ah, sure, why do you want a picture now?"
She held her speechless sister's tiny hand
A sweet, uneasy frown on her little brow.
"You're the most lovely women in this whole land."
"Go 'long with you, you're joking us, we know."
Still she posed for my quick camera shot
Elegant model at a fashion show
As though poverty were not her daily lot.

Grown up now, she must have full woman's grace
Much less poor, courtesy of the EEC,
A slender figure, I think, and a pretty face
Not yet marked by life's anxious misery
Please, God, protect my model's youthful charm
On life's daft journey, keep her free from harm.

—*A. G.*

In Dublin's fair city,
Where the girls are so pretty,
I first set my eyes
On sweet Molly Malone,
She wheeled her wheel-barrow
Through streets broad and narrow,
Crying cockles and mussels,
Alive, alive oh!
Alive, alive oh!
Alive, alive oh!
Crying cockles and mussels
Alive, alive oh!

She was a fishmonger,
But sure 'twas no wonder,
For so was her father and mother before
And they both wheeled their barrow
Through streets broad and narrow
Crying cockles and mussels,
Alive, alive oh!
Alive, alive oh!
Alive, alive oh!
Crying cockles and mussels
Alive, alive oh!

She died of a fever
And no-one could relieve her,
And that was the end of sweet Molly Malone,
But her ghost wheels her barrow
Through streets broad and narrow,
Crying cockles and mussels,
Alive-alive-oh!
Alive, alive oh!
Alive, alive oh!
Crying cockles and mussels
Alive, alive oh!

—*Traditional Dublin song*

KITTY OF COLERAINE

As beautiful Kitty one morning was tripping
With a pitcher of milk from the fair of Coleraine,
When she saw me she stumbled, the pitcher down tumbled.
And all the sweet butter-milk watered the plain.
"Oh what shall I do now? 'Twas looking at you now,
Sure, sure, such a pitcher I'll ne'er meet again!
'Twas the pride of my dairy! Oh Barney MacCleary
You're sent as a plague to the girls of Coleraine!"

—Traditional Irish ballad

I SHALL NOT DIE

I shall not die because of you
O woman though you shame the swan,
They were foolish men you killed,
Do not think me a foolish man.

Why should I leave the world behind
For the soft hand, the dreaming eye,
The crimson lips, the breasts of snow—
It is for these you'd have me die?

Why should I heed the fancy free,
The joyous air, the eye of blue,
The side like foam, the virgin neck?
I shall not die because of you.

The devil take the golden hair!
That maiden look, that voice so gay,
That delicate heel and pillared thigh
Only some foolish man would slay.

O woman though you shame the swan
A wise man taught me all he knew,
I know the crooked ways of love,
I shall not die because of you.

—Anonymous, eighteenth century

Welcome to our wide wild world, wonderchild,
And the waters that work it wilder still
To a life yoked to the One sweet and mild
Who turned death to life on Golgotha hill

May His clear light lead you through gloom and dark
And His white robe promise both peace and fun
May holy oils your flesh for Eucharist mark
And may Mary guard you till home you come

May God Bless you
The Father who made it all
The Son who walked among us
The Spirit who lingers still

May you swim in warm and gentle waves
Under clear skies that match your timeless eyes
May Jesus and Mary keep you sound and safe
And lead you to womanhood, healthy and wise
May the sand move softly beneath your feet
May the angels frolic when you play and sing
May the trees shade you from the summer heat
And may summer sweet surprises always bring
And may God bless you
The Father who created you
The Son who showed you how to live
And the Spirit who loves you

May the lake be smooth beneath your skis
And the winds blow wide your colored sails
May the sand be warm as you take your ease
And God's grace bathe you that never fails
May the sun shine bright on your joyous days
And the rain refresh you through peaceful nights
May summer show you God's wondrous ways
And prepare you for heaven's great delights

Till we meet there
May the God of summertime
Hold you in the palm of His hand
Father, Son, and Holy Spirit

Rest peaceful, small marvel, in your little bed
Be protected from dark terrors of the night
May God's grace linger on your splendid head
And keep you warm till the coming back of light

May Jesus and Mary watch you always
And keep you wise and healthy, safe and sound
Be well loved through your journey's nights and days
Till all of us in peace and joy abound

And may God bless you and keep you, wonderchild,
Always and forever and even after that
Father, Son, and Holy Spirit

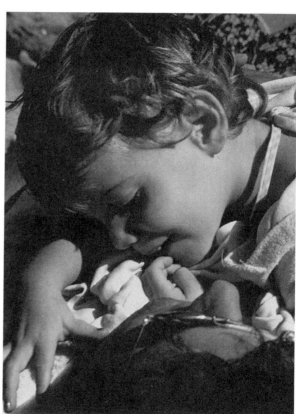

May the autumn leaves carpet beneath your feet
And the angels lead you through the classday maze
May your homecoming time be extra sweet
And your heart warm with Indian summer days
Like Jesus may you grow in wisdom, age, and grace
May you learn to read and write and think and sing
May you swiftly run in knowledge's rapid race
And God's kind love to all your roommates bring

May God hold you in the palm of His hand
Until we meet again
And keep you safe and well
Father, Son, and Holy Spirit

May our holy faith wipe away your tears
And God's love soon restore your smiles
May you heal one another's haunting fears
Because death triumphs for but a little while

May you bear the pain as long as it must last
Since through our cross each must show love's worth
And when the long night of dour grief is past
Remember, in the sunrise, that death is birth

And may the God of the eternal day
Bring you hope and peace
Father, Son, and Holy Spirit

May you sing each note loud and clear
May your diction be articulate and precise
May you survive that curtain-rising fear
And the audience think you're cool as ice

May you remember every single line
And your talents from God always cherish
May you sing in his honor all the time
And may the whole world become your parish

And may the God of Song and Dance bless you
The Father who started the dance
The Son who calls the tune
And the Spirit who plays the pipes

May you be spirited by the water's flow
And dazzle all in your shining Easter dress
And may your life reflect the Christ-candle glow
And the holy oil challenge you to your best

May you sleep peacefully in the Church's care
And awake with eager and laughing heart
Responding to God's offered love affair
Whatever the Lord wants, you'll do your part

And the God who brought you to life in an act of love
And offers you life as a revelation of His love
Bless you and protect you with that love
Father, Son, and Holy Spirit

May Madonna and Child protect this babe
May the child be welcome, girl or boy,
And enter the world healthy and safe
And may Mom and Dad be filled with joy
May they see in their child a hint of immortality
And celebrate with laughter and mirth
That new life is the ultimate reality
For birth is death and death is birth

May Jesus, who was once an unborn babe,
Bless this mother and child
Together with the Father and the Holy Spirit

A HAZEL STICK FOR CATHERINE ANN

The living mother-of-pearl of a salmon
just out of the water

is gone just like that, but your stick
is kept salmon-silver.

Seasoned and bendy,
it convinces the hand

that what you have you hold
to play with and pose with

and lay about with.
But then too it points back to cattle

and spatter and beating
the bars of a gate—

the very stick we might cut
from your family tree.

The living cobalt of an afternoon
dragonfly drew my eye to it first

and the evening I trimmed it for you
you saw your first glow-worm—

all of us stood round in silence, even you
gigantic enough to darken the sky

for a glow-worm.
and when I poked open the grass

a tiny brightening den lit the eye
in the blunt cut end of your stick.

—*Seamus Heaney*

I WON'T MARRY AT ALL

I won't marry a man that is rich
For he'd do nothing but sit in a ditch;
I won't marry at all, at all;
I won't marry at all.

I won't marry a man that is poor,
For he'd go begging from door to door;
I won't marry at all, at all;
I won't marry at all.

I won't marry a man that is old,
For he'd do nothing but fight and scold;
I won't marry at all, at all;
I won't marry at all.

I won't marry a man that is young,
For he'd do nothing but look for fun;
I won't marry at all, at all;
I won't marry at all.

So I'll take my stool and sit in the shade,
For I'm determined to die an old maid;
I won't marry at all, at all;
I won't marry at all.

—Irish ballad, eighteenth century

134

May you grow and prosper in age and grace
And health and faith and all good things
To your mom and dad be always kind
And treasure life as a wondrous gift

May God bless you
The Father from whom all life comes
The Son who came in Bethlehem
And the Spirit who leads the dance

THE INDIFFERENT MISTRESS

She is my love
Though she makes my life a hell
Dearer, though she makes me sick,
Than one who would make me well.

She is my dear
Who has reduced me to a slave,
She'd never let one sigh for me
Or lay a stone on my grave.

She is my treasure
Whose eye is stern with pride,
She'd never put an arm under my head
Or lie at my side.

She is my secret
Who won't speak a word to me,
Who won't listen to anything under the sun
Or turn an eye on me.

—Irish love poem, eighteenth century

RECONCILIATION

Do not torment me, woman,
Let our two minds be as one,
Be my mate in my own land
Where we may live till life is done.

Put your mouth against my mouth
You whose skin is fresh as foam,
Take me in your white embrace
And let us love till kingdom come.

Slender graceful girl, admit
Me soon into your bed,
Discord, pain will disappear
When we stretch there side by side.

For your sweet sake, I will ignore
Every girl who takes my eye,
If it's possible, I implore
You do the same for me.

As I have given from my heart
Passion for which alone I live,
Let me now receive from you
The love you have to give.

—Irish love poem, eighteenth century

Here's a Mollie Woopie story. It tells of the time Mollie Woopie lost all her clout because of some shenanigans perpetrated by football players at her school. Let's listen in to the story, told by a third-generation Irish-American teenager living somewhere in the valleys of county Cook.

Mollie Woopie got in a real lot of trouble recently because of what the really gross boys on the football team did. It really cashed her out. Like totally. Mollie like tells everyone she knows that she will never lift a finger again to help some gross boy out of a problem he made for himself. Not even Joe, her boyfriend. Well, kind of a boyfriend anyway.

Joe laughs when he hears Mollie Woopie say that because everyone knows that Joe is the kind of boy who never gets in trouble—or, as Mollie says, if Joe does get in trouble, no one ever catches him.

Well, anyway, as you know, Mollie is the president of the student body at Mother Mary even though she's only a junior, and everyone says that she like totally runs the school. I mean even the principal admits that she seems to be in charge only because Mollie lets her give a few orders and make a few decisions so she'll feel good.

So anyone who's in trouble first goes to the dean and then to the principal and then to the president and then, when worst comes to worst and everything else has failed, to Mollie Woopie, who, like, tries to persuade the school to give him or her another chance.

She's had a perfect record because, like her father goes, Mollie was a great trial lawyer in an earlier incarnation. You know?

And everyone knows that the kids Mollie gets out of trouble will never do anything wrong ever again because they're afraid of being in trouble with her.

Like totally.

So when the gross senior boys from the football team—I mean like really gross—got in a whole lot of trouble when they had drunk too much after winning the football championship, everyone wondered whether Mollie Woopie would, like, try to get them out of trouble.

You see, Mollie doesn't take on every case. If someone does something really geeky, Mollie says that's his problem and she can't do anything about it.

Well, the football team was really good this year and won the division championship before it lost in the playoffs, like, you know, the Chicago Cubs, right?

But, as the season went on and the team kept winning, some of the senior boys on the team got really stuck up, even worse than senior boys usually do. Mollie thought this was totally gross and didn't go to any of their parties and didn't cheer much at their games.

You see, these retards thought that because they won football games they could do anything they wanted to and nobody would dare to punish them. At first they did geeky little things like writing gross notes on the blackboard. Nobody punished them because, well, like, they were really good football players, you know?

Then they started making fun of teachers, and everyone laughed with them, including the teachers, because the whole school was proud of the team, right? Then they started drinking in cars in the parking lot, and no one liked that, but they kind of pretended not to pay any attention because everyone said they'd settle down after the football season was over.

Mollie Woopie gave them all the cold shoulder, and, you know, no one can give the cold shoulder like she can. But it didn't do any good, because these gross senior boys were not afraid of anyone—not even Mollie Woopie.

Well, the night they won the division, they all got totally drunk and broke into the school and did terrible things. Like they put a bikini on a statue of St. Teresa and trashed the girls' washrooms and wrote like totally gross words on the wall and kidnapped the baby Jesus from the Christmas crib and stole some files from the dean's office and burned them in the back of the chapel and wrecked one of the science labs—I mean really!

And they were so dumb that they got caught because they left their jackets in the lab. Like Mollie said, if Joe had done such gross things he wouldn't be so drunk as to leave behind all kinds of clues.

Joe said they wanted to be caught to prove that no one would dare do anything to them. Well, they were all expelled first thing in the morning. And the president called in the police and made charges against them and told their parents that she'd have the police arrest them if they didn't pay for all the damage.

At first the parents were high and mighty, you know, like some parents are when their darlings are caught doing something wrong; one geeky father said the president was only kidding because these boys were going to win the city championship, and the president said, "You just watch me."

By the end of the day everyone believed the president, and some of the girls were even crying because they had their hearts set on winning. Mollie Woopie said she thought the boys were like totally disgusting. And besides, the gross things they drew on walls weren't even good gross art.

When Mollie said things like that, it usually ended the conversation.

Well, everyone was in despair, so the football coach, who was a good man, though not strict enough, went to Mollie Woopie and begged her to talk to the president. These were good boys, he said. They'd never done anything like that before, and they deserved another chance. They'd clean up the mess, they'd go to the jug till the day after the Last Judgment, they'd clean up the school every night, they'd never drink on school property again or come into the school after they'd been drinking. They'd do volunteer work on weekends. They'd do anything.

It wasn't the championship so much. All of them wanted to go to college, and if they were really thrown out of high school they'd have a hard time getting into a good college. So, would Mollie Woopie beg the president to give them one more chance if they made all the promises she wanted?

No way, said Mollie Woopie. They're like totally gross.

Then the boys came and pleaded with her, and two of them were actually crying because their parents were suffering so much. And it wasn't even the football game—it was college and their families.

Mollie said she'd think about it.

They promised, they swore up and down, they, like, totally gave their words to Mollie Woopie.

So she went to the president, who seemed glad to see her, and they had a long talk, and Mollie said they had been nice boys, even kind of sweet, until they thought they were a big deal because of the football team, and maybe if they made up for everything and paid for everything and promised everything they deserved another chance.

The president goes, "Do you guarantee their good behavior, Mollie Woopie?"

Mollie didn't like to do that because she knew that she'd lose a lot of her clout. But she had pleaded so much she thought she couldn't turn back. So she goes like, "Really!"

Well, you know what happened. The senior boys were put on probation, and they made all kinds of promises, and they went to football practice that night, and everyone cheered for them.

And not a single one came to Mollie Woopie to say "Thanks for using your clout to help us."

"Gross out," she said to Joe.

St. Finian's beat Mother Mary on Saturday forty-four to nothing.

The senior boys got drunk again and smashed all the windows on the west side of the school and trashed the yearbook office, the athletic office, and the president's office.

They were expelled Monday morning.

One of their mothers came to Mrs. Woopie and begged her with tears pouring down her face to ask Mollie to get them out of trouble again.

Mrs. Woopie goes to Mollie, "Do you think you can help them, dear?"

Mollie Woopie goes, "No way. They're like total retards."

"You should help them if you can, dear."

"They're ungrateful space cadets," Mollie goes. "I suppose I'd help them if I could, but because they weren't grateful enough to keep their promises and I've lost all my clout with the president, they're history. Archive them." That night Mollie Woopie cried herself to sleep.

And Mollie Woopie was right, like she always is. Those gross senior boys are history. The archives are the only place in school where you can find them.

People ask me why all the women in my novels are strong. I respond that those are the only kind of women I know. That's an exaggeration. There are weak and passive Irish women too. But our ethnic group seems to produce a disproportionate share of women like Mollie Woopie—strong minds, strong wills, and strong, strong right arms.

On the whole they're the best kind. Or so it seems to most of their long-suffering men folk, such as Joe, Mollie Woopie's boyfriend. A woman who is strong yet vulnerable seems to be the ideal lover—strong enough to take care of you, vulnerable enough to need your care.

We Irish are not so fond of passive, clinging, dependent women—and we have them, like every other culture, though perhaps not so many of them, because it is not a cultural ideal.

I'll confess I find such women a terrible burden and am happy when they finally creep away and leave me alone.

The other side of the Irish woman picture is that of the strong woman who suppresses her vulnerability—as she often had to do in the culture's tragic history. A human being, man or woman, who has crushed every bit of softness in his or her character is dominating but not appealing, strong but not lovable, tough but not affectionate.

Libera nos, Domine.

It has been said—not altogether accurately, if you ask me—that Ireland is

run by the women and the priests and that the priests run the women.

The truth is that the women run the priests too, and so do the children, for whom the priests are pushovers, especially the girl children.

So if anyone runs the Irish, it's the girl children. People like Mollie Woopie. The world could do worse.

Whence this Irish tradition of take-charge women?

It would not be accurate to say that the pre-Christian Celts comprised a matriarchal society. Despite the wild claims of some feminist pseudo-scholarship, there does not seem ever to have been a matriarchal society. The truth for Ireland is more modest. Women had far more rights in the Celtic lands than they did in the Mediterranean world: they could own property on their own, choose their own husband, terminate a marriage on their own initiative, enter a "trial marriage" of a year and a day and refuse to renew, inherit property, and even act as head of the clan in the husband's absence.

You didn't push them around, and you still don't.

A number of years ago an English Gallup poll did a survey of attitudes toward the role of women in the common market countries. On some thirty-two measures of "feminism" the Irish were either first or second in all but one. Second-highest were the Danes, who shared first or second place with the Irish on most items.

I am not denying that the women in Ireland are the objects of sexism and male exploitation. I'm merely asserting that they are less exploited than anyone else.

In this country the highest support for the ordination of women comes from

Irish-Catholic men over age forty-five (even more than from any demographic group of women). Why is this virtuous attitude shared by Irish men of a certain age?

'Tis easy to answer: by that time in life the men are already surrounded by sacred women—mother, sister, wife, daughters. So ordain them—it won't give them any more power!

If the strength of our women is one of the greatest assets of Irish culture, it also creates the most poignant problem of intimacy between men and women who are products of that culture—the yearning of Irish women for men who are strong enough to be a match for them and the repeated testing of their menfolk to determine whether they are indeed that strong. It can be a pleasant exchange, but, alas, it is often unpleasant. That, however, is a subject for my novels, not for this book. Maybe, in a way, for all of my novels.

The Irish are also kid freaks, both in Ireland and in America. In this country only the Irish Catholics and the blacks now have families that deviate significantly from the national mean—and there is reason to believe that the black difference can be explained by economic factors. The Irish are more likely to reject the Catholic birth control doctrine than other Catholics, so the size of their families can't be attributed to acceptance of that teaching.

Similarly, in Ireland, while birth control is readily available and generally accepted (despite the bishops), and while the Irish birthrate is only somewhat higher than that in the rest of the European community, the Irish seem to delight in their children—who are handsome, contentious, and delightful.

Mollie Woopie and Joe in the making!

There are Irish men too, but they're not as important as Irish women, not at all, at all. Still, I thought we'd show you some pictures of them.

VII
A Few of Us Still Around

May the saints be surprised at your success!

—*West Cork wish*

May the strength of three be on your journey with you!

To the health of your enemies' enemies!

May God hold you in the palm of His hand—and not squeeze!

May we all be here next year to drink this toast again!

May your soul be in heaven half an hour before the devil knows you're dead!

—*Irish proverbs*

May Brigid, Patrick, and Colum smooth your trip
And all the other saints keep a watchful eye
So you not lose your balance and never slip
May Mary's gentle love be always nigh
May the Spirit's guidance you never lack
And on your journey let nothing go awry
May Brendan and Kiernan bring you safely back
But a moment after you've said good-bye
And may the God of journeys go with you on the way
And quickly bring you home again
Father, Son, and Holy Spirit

May the door swing open with cheerful charm
And the old familiar mutt jump and bark
May everyone you love wait with welcome arms
And the light of friends chase away the dark
May Mary keep your home from all wicked harm
May you sing and dance and talk and play all night
May your grace and kindness all fear disarm
May you wait a day before your first good fight
May the God of homecomings welcome you home
Each day and at the end of all our days
And forevermore, Father, Son, and Holy Spirit

May the tunes of angels echo in your brain
May heaven's rhythms tap your twitching feet
May you sing along with Mary's sweet refrain
And may you sway to the Lord's demanding beat
Dance with all the lovers He has taught your song
And, sure, spin with Himself at every chance
Whenever He invites you all night long
Never say no to the Lord of the Dance
May the Lord of the Dance bless you and lead you in
The dance, Father, Son, and Holy Spirit

May the Good Shepherd protect you in

Ups and downs
Ins and outs
Bounds and rebounds
Highs and lows
Comings and goings
Heat and cold
Darkness and light
Joy and sorrow
Good times and bad times
Daytimes and nighttimes
Short times and long times
Old times and new times

May He be with you

At home and abroad
On the road and at rest
In storm and flood
In drought and desert
In peace and conflict
In doubt and assurance
In sickness and health
In pain and triumph

May the Good Shepherd walk with you always
Until it is time to return home

And may God bless you, Father, Son, and Holy Spirit

May Jesus and Mary
Protect you from
Falling stars
Crowded bars
Hateful words
Tiresome nerds
Hairpin turns
Dying ferns
Things that go bump in the night
Prices that go out of sight
Wind shear twist
Sunburn risk
Plunging stocks
Broken locks
Bears defeats
Muddy cleats
Russian flus
Winter blues
Ice-cold feet
Love's retreat
Noisy teens
Worn-out springs
Early burnout
Unfriendly clout
Traffic jams
The L.A. Rams
Bitter moods
Too rich food
Too much drink
Leaky sinks
Windchill sting
And every other
Evil thing

And God cherish you
In the palm of His hand
And Bless you now and always,
Father, Son, and Holy Spirit

155

May it be a grand day for all of you
Be ye Irish or as Patrick as you'd like to be
May your jars be limited to just a few
May you revel in God's great diversity
In a land where Moslem, Protestant, Catholic, Jew
Enjoy a constitutional variety
Modestly raise a quiet cry and hue
To give thanks for peaceful ethnicity
And praise for pluralism's brightest jewel
Drink joyous toasts in all sobriety
To the one from many 'neath red, white, and blue

And may God bless you this glorious day
The Father who holds the world together
The Son who walked among us
And the Spirit who makes each of us unique

As I look at the Irish faces in this book—friends and family, strangers and lovers, old and young, happy and sad—I wonder what might identify them as Irish.

There is one non-Irish face in the book. I wonder if anyone can pick it out.

Some Jewish friends of mine went to Ireland recently and fell in love with the country. They now claim that they can spot an Irish face in a crowd almost as surely as one of us can. I'm not so sure about that, but I don't argue. Better that they think they're almost Irish!

To be sober about it, there are many different kinds of Irish visages—red hair, black hair, blond hair; fair skin, dark skin, freckled skin; blue eyes, gray eyes, green eyes, brown eyes; pre-Celt, Celt Dane, Norman.

Yet there are types within that pool that are easily recognizable—not that the Irish have a monopoly on them. But the Irish have a disproportionate number of them.

On his honeymoon in Italy Chicago mayor Richard M. Daley was taken by many of the natives to be Italian. Yet we say of him, What face could be more Irish, what smile more Irish?

So we interpret faces as having a certain ethnic quality based on what we think we already know about the background of the person.

Yet there are still faces in this book that one could identify as having their origins in the Sod with a 99 percent probability of being right.

Maybe we should have a contest to determine which is the most Irish face.

I myself chose the eleven faces on pages 160–170 in no particular order of their Irishness.

If I were determined to read into pictures what I think ought to be there, I would propose that these faces reflect in a special way the themes of my musings—dreamers and mystics, talkers and writers, lovers and friends, celebrants and disputants, women and kids.

All of them are men, women, and children who are acutely, if often preconsciously, aware of the preciousness of the world, of the possibility of surprise, of lurking magic and mystery, of the fragility and glory of human life.

161

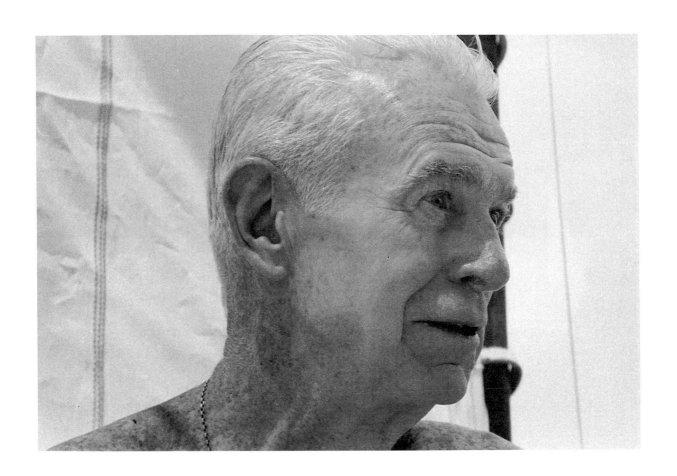

All of which reminds me of a story, Irish-American like the other stories and the blessings in this book, but set in the ancient Kingdom of Kerry:

Once upon a time, long, long ago, there was a great king in the Kingdom of Kerry in the west of Ireland named Fergus MacDiarmud UiDonal (McDermot O'Donnell, if you wish). He was a great and good and wise and brave king, and he ruled his people justly and wisely. There was peace and prosperity in the whole Kingdom of Kerry during the half century he ruled, and all called him Fergus the Good.

But at last he grew old, as we all must, and his health failed, and he knew he was going to die. So he summoned his councillors and his warriors and his poets and his priests and ordered his servants to carry him out to the meadow in front of his ring fort. There he said a tearful good-bye to his wife of fifty years and his children and his grandchildren and even his little great-granddaughter, a blond-haired toddler about three years old.

Then, as life was slipping away, he looked up at the green hills and the blue sky and the golden fields and the silver lakes of the Kingdom of Kerry and loved all the kingdom and all its people. Finally, just as he commended his soul to God, he scooped up in his right hand a clump of thick, rich Kerry turf.

Well, the next thing he knew he was at the big gold and silver gates of a big city with great ivory walls. In front of the gate was a man dressed in white robes and wearing a triple crown, sitting at an IBM PC AT computer, with a fishing rod next to it.

"And who would you be," says your man Simon Peter, alias Pope Peter I, "and what would you be wanting from us?"

"Well," says the king, respectful but not afraid, "I'm King Fergus MacDiarmud UiDonal, king of Kerry, and if it's all the same to you, I wouldn't mind if you let me into that city."

All the time the king was holding the clump of Kerry turf behind his back.

"UiDonal, is it? Well, now, let me see." Your man called up his Lotus 1-2-3 and punched in an entry. He made a mistake—infallibility does not apply to operating a PC—corrected it, and touched the ENTER key. "Ah, yes, Your Majesty, we have a long record on you here in our data base. And most of it's good, very good indeed. A few wild moments when you were young, but sure, Himself forgave them long before you did. To tell you the truth, me bucko, there's no purgatory at all, at all for you."

"Well, I'm grateful to you for that, God knows," King Fergus said with a great west-of-Ireland sigh.

The pope punched in an escape code, and, pretty as you please, the great gold and silver gates began to swing open.

"Ah, just a minute now, Your Majesty," your man says as King Fergus slipped by him. "What's that you're holding in your hand?"

" 'Tis nothing at all."

" 'Tis too." Peter punched a Control C, and the gates stopped swinging. "What have you got there?"

"Sure, 'tis nothing but a wee bit of Kerry turf, to remind me of home, if you take my meaning."

"I take your meaning, all right, but you can't have it. Against the rules. No one enters the kingdom of heaven save with empty hands."

"Well, Your Reverence, if that's the lay of the land"—King Fergus was not the kind of man you'd want to fool with when his back was up—"I'd just as soon not go in if I can't bring me piece of Kerry turf with me."

"Rules is rules," your man insists.

"Then I'll just wait out here."

The pope put in a hurry-up call, murmured discreetly into the phone, listened, said "Aye," and hung up.

A minute later the big gold and silver gates swung open, and out strode the Lord God Himself. He's ten feet tall and has long blond hair and looks like a linebacker for the Chicago Bears. He embraced the king, slapped him on the back, and boomed out in a rich baritone voice, "Faith, it's good to see you, Fergus me boy; we've been waiting up for a long time for you. Come right in. We'll have a wee talk about how difficult it is to be a king. Just toss aside that little bit of Kerry turf and come on in. There'll be the singing and the dancing and the telling of tales all night long."

Your man Fergus MacDiarmud UiDonal was moved by this warm greeting, but not moved enough. Like I say, when he got his back up, he could be a difficult man.

"Saving Your Reverence," the king says, "I'll not be coming in unless I can bring me little handful of Kerry turf. Sure, it won't do any harm at all, at all."

Well, the Lord God seemed greatly disappointed. "Faith, we can't let you do that, Fergus me friend. Rules is rules. You can't come into the kingdom of heaven save with empty hands. I don't make the rules, you know. Well, actually I do, but that's one we just can't change, if you take my meaning."

"I can wait," the king says, real stubborn-like.

So the Lord God sighed a great west-of-Ireland sigh and walked slowly back into the city.

And the great gold and silver gates clanked shut.

"You might go around to the back and see if Herself will let you in," says your man Simon Peter. "Sure, She gets a lot of folk in that way, and Herself having a lot of clout. But that's one rule even She won't bend."

"If it's all the same to you," the king said, still real stubborn, "I'll wait here in the rain."

Didn't I tell you it was raining outside of the heavenly city? Well, of course it was.

The Lord God is devious and will stop at nothing to get us into the heavenly city. So He disguised Himself as an Irish countryman—you know, the gray suit that hasn't been cleaned or pressed for forty years, the old brown sweater, the dirty tie, the big galoshes, the cap pulled down over his head—and put a big Havana cigar in his mouth. Then He slipped out of the gates and stood next to King Fergus MacDiarmud UiDonal, watching in silence as the mists rose up over the bogs.

"Have one," said the Lord God, offering a cigar to the king. "They don't hurt you up here."

"Aye, don't mind if I do," says King Fergus.

" 'Tis a bad night."

" 'Tis."

" 'Tis warm and comfy inside."

"Is it now?"

" 'Tis."

They both sighed together.

"We have some fine Jameson's and the best Guinness in the cosmos inside. They don't hurt you up here, either."

"Is that true?"

" 'Tis."

They sighed again.

"You could come in and have a drop of Jameson's by the fire, if only you will get rid of that handful of dirt you've got there."

"I know who you are," King Fergus exploded. "You're no countryman; you're the Lord God. And You ought to be ashamed of Yourself with all them tricks. I'll not come in without me Kerry turf."

"Ah, but we can't allow that, don't you see. Sure, no one comes into the Kingdom of Heaven—"

"Save with empty hands," the king finishes for him.

So the Lord God, dejected-like, walked back into the heavenly city.

And the big gold and silver gates clanked shut.

The next trick the Lord God pulled was to disguise Himself as a wee blond colleen, with a few freckles on her nose, looking just like the king's great-granddaughter.

And the colleen who was really the Lord God slipped up to King Fergus MacDiarmud UiDonal and says to him, "Oh, King Fergus, they're having a wonderful party inside for all the little kids, but I can't go unless I can find a grown-up to take me. Would you ever think of being me grown-up?"

Well, the king was moved, let me tell you. "You can't find another grown-up?"

"Not at all, at all."

"Well . . ."

"Just put down that silly old turf and we can both go to the party."

"I'll not be taken in by Your tricks," the king shouted. "I know who You are. You're not a wee lass; You're the Lord God in disguise. And I won't come in without me Kerry turf, and don't repeat the rules—I know them by heart . . ."

So King Fergus and the Lord God and your man Simon Peter all said together, "No one enters the Kingdom of Heaven save with empty hands."

And with tears in her eyes, the little blond colleen with the freckles on her nose went back into the heavenly city.

And the big gold and silver gates clanked shut.

Well, the night got darker and the rain colder and the Kerry turf more crumbly. And King Fergus began to think about it.

Sure, Fergus, he says to himself, a prize amadon you are. This isn't Kerry; it's the Kingdom of Heaven. They make their own laws here, and they're not going to change them for you, even if you wait till all eternity. You've been counting on sneaking through those gates since you were a wee lad. Isn't it time you'd be after coming to your senses?

So with the loudest sigh all day, doesn't he stroll over to St. Peter's desk and toss the turf on the ground?

"Begging Your Reverence's pardon, but there's no sense in fighting the Lord God, is there now?"

"Not at all, at all," says your man Simon Peter happily. He punched in the escape code, making no mistake this time. The big gold and silver gates of heaven clanked open. "There's no one goes through those gates save with empty hands."

"Aye," says the king, feeling like he was pretty much the fool, if you take my meaning, but still mourning for his lost Kerry turf.

And so he walked through the big gold and silver gates. And do you know what he found inside?

Do you?

Ah, you don't.

Sure you do.

Well, I'll tell you. Inside, waiting for King Fergus MacDiarmud UiDonal was . . . what?

The green hills and the blue skies and the golden fields and the silver lakes and the whole Kingdom of Kerry!

And sometimes people take my picture too.